Python: Building BIG Apps

level 3

Chris Roffey

CAMBRIDGE
UNIVERSITY PRESS

University Printing House, Cambridge CB2 8BS, United Kingdom

One Liberty Plaza, 20th Floor, New York, NY 10006, USA

477 Williamstown Road, Port Melbourne, VIC 3207, Australia

4843/24, 2nd Floor, Ansari Road, Daryaganj, Delhi – 110002, India

79 Anson Road, #06–04/06, Singapore 079906

Cambridge University Press is part of the University of Cambridge.

It furthers the University's mission by disseminating knowledge in the pursuit of education, learning and research at the highest international levels of excellence.

www.cambridge.org
Information on this title: www.cambridge.org/9781107666870

© Cambridge University Press 2013

This publication is in copyright. Subject to statutory exception and to the provisions of relevant collective licensing agreements, no reproduction of any part may take place without the written permission of Cambridge University Press.

First published 2013
20 19 18 17 16 15 14 13 12 11 10 9 8

Printed in Poland by Opolgraf

A catalogue record for this publication is available from the British Library

ISBN 978-1-107-66687-0 Paperback

Cambridge University Press has no responsibility for the persistence or accuracy of URLs for external or third-party internet websites referred to in this publication, and does not guarantee that any content on such websites is, or will remain, accurate or appropriate.

Contents

Introduction ... 4

Chapter 1: Can you guess my password? ... 7

Chapter 2: Objects, classes and factories ... 17

The MyPong Project ... 32

Chapter 3: Creating the Table ... 34

Chapter 4: Making the Ball ... 51

Chapter 5: Building the Bats ... 69

Chapter 6: The rules and scoring ... 91

Bonus Chapter: Two more games ... 106

Taking things further ... 120

Appendix: Some key bits of information ... 123

Glossary and index ... 126

Quick Quiz answers ... 131

Acknowledgements ... 132

Introduction

Who is this book for?

This book is the Level 3 core book in the Coding Club series. Before reading this, you should have either read *Coding Club, Python: Next Steps* or have become familiar with Python 3 and learned about variables, while loops, lists and tuples. This book is aimed at coders with a little bit of previous programming experience.

Why should you choose this book?

Building larger programs and applications can seem daunting. As well as sorting out the normal details and algorithms, the big picture has to be maintained. This book helps you to see your way through the big picture – it shows you how to break your applications up into manageable chunks that are logical, and even better, reusable. To do this you are given an introduction to a style of programming called object oriented programming (OOP). This is a great way to program but might seem a little more complicated at first than the way you have learned to code in the level 1 and 2 books.

At this stage in your coding it is important that you are introduced to classes and objects. This is because you will certainly want to use other people's classes, and to do this effectively a little understanding goes a long way. What is special about this book is how the explanations are rooted in the real world and use analogies that you will understand. The code is also built so that it mirrors real objects whenever possible. This is so that when you go on to write your own applications you will be able to imagine how to convert real objects into coded objects.

What you will need

Any type of computer can run Python 3. If yours does not already have it installed, there is a section on the companion website (www.codingclub.co.uk) that guides you through installing IDLE and Python 3. This only takes about 5 minutes, and is all you require to get started.

So that you do not have to do too much typing and do not get lost in the bigger projects, there are start files and, if you need them, finished files for all the projects in the book in one easily downloadable zip file. The website also has answers to the puzzles and challenges to help you if you get stuck.

How to use this book

The ideal way to use this book is to read everything carefully and build all the main projects in order. At the end of each chapter there are further ideas, and challenges that you can think of as 'mini quests'. Some readers will want to work through them all so that they understand everything all the time. Some of you will probably prefer to rush through and get to the end. Which approach is best? The one you are most comfortable with. However, if you are being guided by a teacher, you should trust their judgement so that they can help you in the best possible way.

There are four ways in which this book tries to help you to learn:

1. Typing out the code – this is important as it encourages you to work through the code a line at a time (like computers do) and will help you to remember the details in the future.
2. Finding and fixing errors – error messages in Python give you some clues as to what has gone wrong. Solving these problems yourself will help you to become a better programmer. To avoid feeling bored and frustrated though, the code can be downloaded from the companion website www.codingclub.co.uk
3. Experimenting – feel free to experiment with the code you write. See what else you can make it do. If you try all of the challenges, puzzles and ideas, and generally play with the code, this will help you learn how to write code like a pro.
4. Finally, this book will not only provide the code to build some pretty cool, short projects – it will also teach you how the programs were designed. You can then use the same methods to design your own applications.

A word of warning

You may be tempted to simply get the code off the website instead of typing it yourself. If you do, you will probably find that you cannot remember how to write code so easily later. In this book you will only be asked to type small chunks of code at a time – remember that this will help you understand every detail of each of your programs.

Chapter 1
Can you guess my password?

This book assumes that you have read *Coding Club: Python Basics*. If you have not, you should at least understand what variables and functions are and know how to use IDLE in both interactive mode and script mode. In this first chapter you will recall some of this by making a very simple application called 'Guess My Password'. You will then have revised:

- variables

- if, elif and else

- functions

- while loops

- modules

- using IDLE's script mode.

Guess My Password

The game is going to start by asking the player to guess my password. The app then waits for the player's input, which is stored in a **variable**. Finally, the player's input will be compared with the computer's own secret password. If the guess is correct the player is congratulated, if not, a random message is supplied and then the player is asked to try again.

As in the previous *Coding Club* books, you will use **IDLE**, an example of an **IDE**. You can start by opening IDLE and then choosing *New Window* from the *File* menu. This gets you into IDLE's **script mode**. It is a good idea to now re-arrange the windows so that the **interactive mode** console and new window are next to each other and both can be seen at the same time (Figure 1.1).

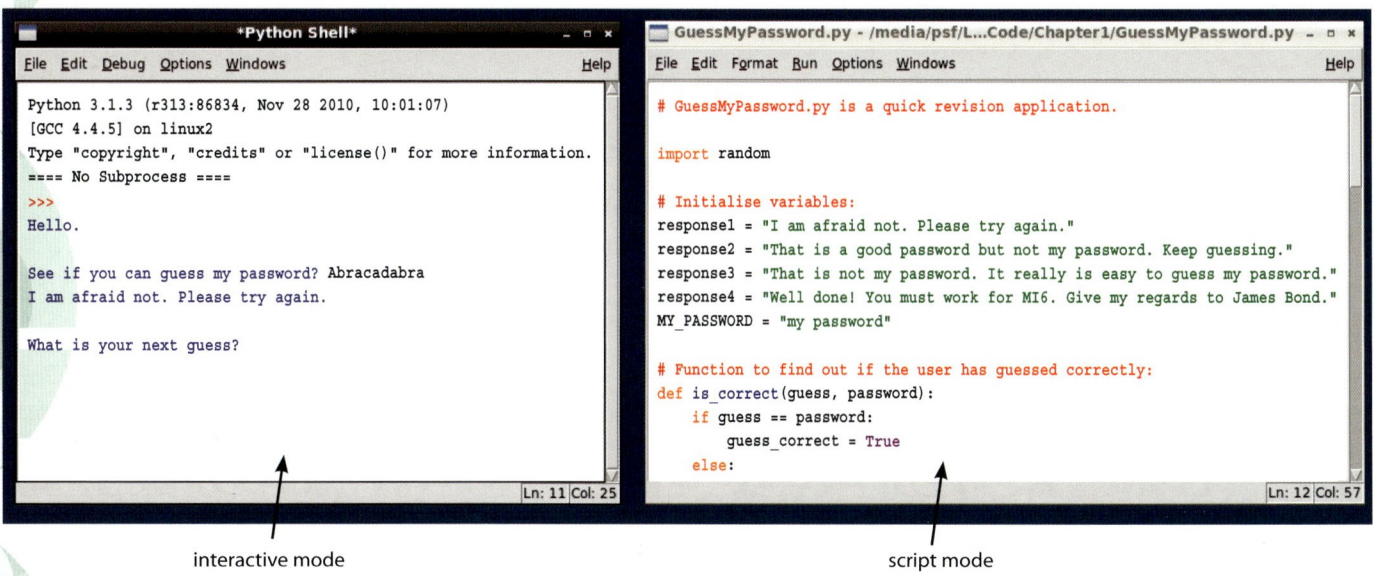

Figure 1.1 A simple IDLE arrangement.

Copy the code from Code Box 1.1 and save the file to your Python Code folder as `GuessMyPassword.py`. You may not have a Python Code folder so you might need to create one first. Choose a sensible place to save this, such as your Documents folder.

Code Box 1.1

```python
# GuessMyPassword.py is a quick revision application.

import random

# Initialise variables:
response1 = "I am afraid not. Please try again."
response2 = "That is a good password but not my password. Keep guessing."
response3 = "That is not my password. It really is easy to guess my password."
response4 = "Well done! You must work for MI6. Give my regards to James Bond."
MY_PASSWORD = "my password"
```

Analysis of Code Box 1.1

Comments

Comments appear in red in IDLE; these are aimed at humans only and begin with the hash symbol #.

Modules

A **module** is a collection of useful functions and data in one place. Sometimes we will want to write our own. Modules have to be imported before they can be used. In this app the `random` module is imported so that it can be used later in the program.

Variables

These are labels we make to allow us to access data. We create a variable by giving it a name and then assign data to it using the **equals operator**. Good programmers begin their variable names with lowercase letters and make them descriptive. The name for a **constant** is all in capitals.

You have just created five **string** type variables and labeled them `response1`, `response2`, `response3`, `response4` and `MY_PASSWORD`.

`MY_PASSWORD` is a constant – it does not change.

Functions

A **function** is a piece of code that can be used again and again. You can already use any of the many functions that are built into Python. You can also make your own. Functions are created with the `def` keyword. Here is the code for a function that finds out if the guess is the correct password.

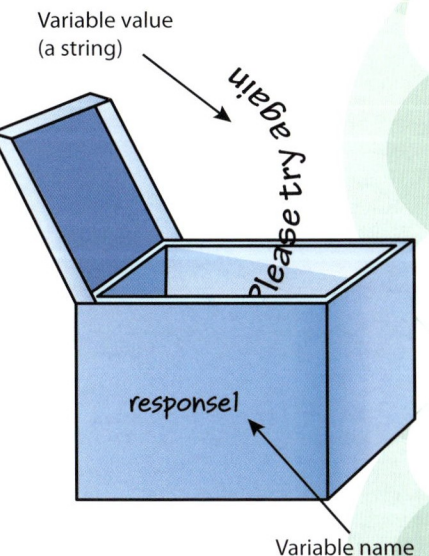

Figure 1.2 A variable called `response1` storing a string.

Code Box 1.2

```python
# Function to find out if the user has guessed correctly:
def is_correct(guess, password):
    if guess == password:
        guess_correct = True
    else:
        guess_correct = False
    return guess_correct
```

Have you saved yet? You should try and remember to do so after entering each Code Box.

Add the code from Code Box 1.2 to your `GuessMyPassword.py` file. The `is_correct()` function has to be passed an **argument** called `guess` and another argument called `password`. The function then compares the two strings. If they are the same, the function sets the `guess_correct` variable to `True`, if not it sets it to `False`. Finally the function will **return** `True` or `False` – depending on the state the `guess_correct` variable is in. A variable that only stores the **values** `True` or `False` is called a **boolean variable**.

User input

To get user input from the keyboard we use Python's `input()` function which waits for the user to type some text and press the enter key. If we want to be able to access the input later we need to assign it to a variable like this:

```
user_input = input()
```

Chapter 1: Can you guess my password?

The function can also take an argument, usually a string, which can act as an output message. This appears on the screen and then the program waits for the user's input:

```
user_input = input("Please type some input: ")
```

Now we are able to access the input, for example, in a print function:

```
print(user_input)
```

We use the `input()` function three times in this program, in two different ways. Now it is time to finish the program by adding the code from Code Box 1.3 to your `GuessMyPassword.py` file. As you type, think carefully about what each line does.

This program contains one of those jokes that are far more fun to tell than to hear.

Code Box 1.3

```
# Start the game:
print("Hello.\n")
users_guess = input("See if you can guess my password?")

# Use our function:
true_or_false = is_correct(users_guess,MY_PASSWORD)

# Run the game until the user is correct:
while true_or_false == False:
    computer_response = random.randint(1, 3)
```

```python
        if computer_response == 1:
            print(response1)
        elif computer_response == 2:
            print(response2)
        else:
            print(response3)

        # Collect the user's next guess:
        users_guess = input("\nWhat is your next guess?")

        # Use our function again:
        true_or_false = is_correct(users_guess, MY_PASSWORD)

# End the game:
print(response4)
input("\n\n\nPress RETURN to exit.")
```

Analysis of Code Box 1.3

Hopefully you can remember how a **while loop** works, as described in *Coding Club: Python Basics*. If not, do not worry as it is fairly obvious what is going on. The code that is indented after

```
while true_or_false == False:
```

forms a block of code. This code keeps running until the `true_or_false` variable is `True`.

`random.randint(1, 3)` generates a random number between one and three. The `randint()` function is from the `random` library so it is necessary to use the **dot operator** to tell our application where to find it.

Many computer languages use the structure:

```
if: [do something]
elseif: [do something else]
else: [do something different again]
```

`elif` is Python's version of `elseif`. You can have as many `elif` clauses as you wish but they must be preceded by an `if` clause and must end with an `else` clause.

Delving Deeper

Writing less code

Coders love finding ways of performing the same task with less code. Hopefully you have found the function in Code Box 1.2 easy to understand and follow. It is logical. There is, however, a lot of unnecessary code in it because we can simply use **comparative operators** to compare two variables and return `True` if they are the same and `False` if not. Hence the whole function in Code Box 1.2 can be replaced with this:

```python
def is_correct(guess, password):
    return guess == password
```

Try it out yourself and see that it still works.

Chapter summary

In this chapter you have revised:

- variables
- if, elif and else clauses
- functions
- while loops
- modules and used the Python's random module
- how to use IDLE's script mode to write and keep your own programs.

As this is a revision chapter, you can now just play with this application if you want. If you feel you need some practice, try the ideas below.

Idea 1

Change all the variables so they are a little more helpful and give a clue. (**Hint:** "Read the question carefully" would be a good clue.)

Idea 2

Make the app a little more useful by enabling the player to respond "yes" to, "Do you give up?" This will need a separate message (`response5` perhaps?) that is triggered after the player has guessed three times. (**Hint**: set a counter variable in the while loop.) Finally, if the player gives up, tell them the password.

An answer and all the source code for this book can be downloaded from the companion website www.codingclub.co.uk. One answer (there are many different ways to solve these problems) is in the Chapter 1 folder in the Answers file and is called `Ch1-Idea2.py`.

I know the password.

Chapter 2
Objects, classes and factories

By the end of this chapter you will have the essential knowledge to start our big project – writing the MyPong application. This chapter is important for another reason – you will be introduced to a particular way of programming called **object-oriented programming (OOP)**. This is one way of coping with the complexity of writing big programs. You are not going to learn everything there is to know about OOP but you will gain a foundation and understand how classes and methods can be built.

There is far more in this chapter about how to design programs than about actually writing them. After you have finished working your way through this book, you will hopefully be starting to think about how to design your own programs rather than just writing the ones that are suggested. The bonus chapter illustrates how well-designed code can quickly be adapted to make new applications.

In this chapter you are going to:

- learn how to design classes
- learn how to make objects from classes
- start to build your own module
- learn how to design larger programs one bit at a time.

Big programs

If we sat down and wanted to build ourselves a car (a real one, as in Figure 2.1) we might not even know where to start. How about starting with the engine? An engine manufacturer does not need to know anything about wheels or windscreen wipers or how to make seats – the engine manufacturer makes engines. A car manufacturer does not need to know how an engine is made; they just need to know how to attach a car to it. A car builder can also get a wheel from one company and a tyre from another company – as long as they fit.

Figure 2.1 McLaren 12C – a very pretty car!

A complex computer program, such as an email application or a video game, can also be very difficult to build because it is also made of many parts. However, just like the car, large applications do not have to be built all at once. The latest video games are often made up of millions of lines of code. If they were built as one program, can you imagine how hard it would be to find a typing mistake? And believe me, everyone makes typing mistakes. The way this problem is avoided is by building little bits at a time.

There are several ways to do this. One of these is to use OOP, which builds programs out of coded objects! The great thing about this is that if you build the **objects** in the correct way, you can make libraries of these objects. These objects can be re-used again in other applications. You can of course do a lot of this with functions but learning about objects and **classes** will help you better understand other people's code. The popular `PyGame` library and **tkinter** both use classes.

Classes

Our first task is to look at a problem and work out how it can be separated into smaller tasks and objects. You have just learned that we build libraries of objects. This is not entirely true. We build libraries of classes. A class is better than an object, because it can act as a **factory** for making objects.

Instead of explaining with a complex situation, let's take something very simple – a cat.

There are many ways to build a Cat class. Here is one:

Code Box 2.1

```python
class Cat:
    def speak(self):
        print("Meow!")

    def drink(self):
        print("The cat drinks its milk.")
        print("The cat takes a nap.")
```

Open a new window in IDLE and type in the code from Code Box 2.1. Save this as `cat.py` in your Python folder.

Analysis of Code Box 2.1

The first thing to note is that we use the `class` keyword and that the class name, `Cat`, starts with a capital. The indented code after the colon belongs to the class. Inside the class we have provided two methods. Methods are very similar to functions except that they belong to a class.

Remember, this is like a factory. Now, you will learn how to send it orders to build some objects – in this case, some cats!

> ### Delving Deeper
>
> **What is the difference between a method and a function?**
>
> A **method** is just a special function that we make in a class.
>
> Computer scientists might get upset with us calling classes 'factories' as this word has another meaning in advanced OOP. They would prefer us to describe classes as *templates* or *blueprints*. You will find it a lot easier to think of classes as factories though.
>
> If you think of classes as factories, you can understand that by requiring a method to have `self` as an argument, you tell the computer that the method will be available to each of the objects made by the factory.

Modules

By storing class files such as `cat.py` in one folder they become a module! Any other Python files in the same folder can use them with a simple import **statement**:

```
import cat
```

There are other special modules in the Python library that can be used. You have already done this once.

> **Quick Quiz 2.1**
>
> Can you remember which module we used before?

main.py

So far we cannot do anything with the Cat class. Have you tried to run it? Not a lot happens does it?

Open a new window in IDLE and type in the code from Code Box 2.2. Then save this new file as `main.py`. Notice `cat.py` is imported at the beginning of the code which gives our program access to the Cat class. The file that you have just created is where you will start to run the program, which is why it is called `main.py`.

Wow, we have made our very own module. OK, so it only has one class in it – but it's a start.

Chapter 2: Objects, classes and factories

Code Box 2.2

```
import cat

# create an instance of a cat, named Romeo
romeo = cat.Cat()

# play with Romeo
romeo.speak()
romeo.drink()
```

Analysis of Code Box 2.2

```
romeo = cat.Cat()
```

This is where we order an object from our cat factory. Computer scientists say: "We have made an **instance** of the Cat class." They might even say that we have **instantiated** a cat object. Romeo is the object and it is created by the Cat class (hence the capital letter). The Cat class is in `cat.py` so we tell `main.py` where to look with the dot operator. The dot is used to link the class with its location. In non-coding language, this line of code translates as:

'Create an object called Romeo using the cat factory found in the `cat.py` file.'

Thus we have a cat! And he is called Romeo! All done with one line of code.

Romeo has all the methods that were built by its factory, the Cat class, available to him. To access them we call them using the dot operator again:

```
romeo.speak()    # calls romeo's speak method
romeo.drink()    # calls romeo's drink method
```

If you have not played with Romeo yet, you can do so now! To play with Romeo you simply save and run `main.py`. It must be in the same folder as `cat.py`.

Improving the Cat class

Warning: There are a lot of selfs in this section!

When calling a function we send it arguments in the brackets like this:

```
times_tables(12, 12)
```

This function is from *Python Basics* and calling it would print out the 12 times table up to $12 \times 12 = 144$. Objects can do this too. We could supply a name for example:

```
romeo = cat.Cat("Romeo")
```

Our Cat class will now need to be re-written though. This is not done in quite the same way as it is in a function. It is done in a special method called a **constructor**.

Constructors have a special bit of code that you will see quite often from now on. It looks a little bit frightening at first but it is always the same – you will get used to it:

```
def __init__(self, name):
```

It always has the `self` argument to make sure that everyone understands that this method is going to be available to each object built by this class. Next we must list the other arguments that we want to pass to the constructor. In the above example the other argument needed is `name`.

Now let's pause. You may not have been confused by the `init` surrounded by two underscores on each side of it; you may have noticed that this is actually a method because it has `def` at the beginning and a colon at the end; you may be a very clever coder! Most students need a little encouragement at this stage – listen to Mr Campbell.

Now back to work! In this special method called a constructor we have to create a `self.name` variable from `name` (yes that's right, so that it is available to the object created by this class). We then will use this new variable, `self.name`, in our methods.

We are adding `self.` to the front of all the variable names that are going to be available to our objects and not simply to the class. This is why we end up with a lot of `self`s!

We have nearly finished the new theory. After this section it is only a few more examples and then you have learned the basics for starting your project.

Delving Deeper

When we build classes, we write methods that will be available to the objects we build (create instances of). In a game of snooker, there may be several balls with different locations. Each one has a `find_location()`

method that refers only to itself, even though it has been built from the same class. This is why the methods in our class have `self` passed to them as an argument. It is even cleverer than this though.

Programmatically the objects do, in actual fact, refer back to the class code for the method but each object keeps track of its own data. It is as if each object has been built with its own methods that are specific to it alone. It is as if the methods act independently of the other objects built by the same factory. This is just what we would wish for when we build objects, and it is all done with one argument – `self`.

Open a new window in IDLE and copy the code from Code Box 2.3. Save it as `cat2.py`. Compare this with `cat.py` (Code Box 2.1) to see how we use the new variable `self.name` created in the constructor. Yes, that is all this constructor code has done: it has given you a new variable that you can use! As before, this class does not run anything. It is just a factory, but you are about to see how useful factories are.

Code Box 2.3

```
class Cat:
    # constructor:
    def __init__(self, name):
        self.name = name

    def speak(self):
        print(self.name, " says Meow")

    def drink(self):
        print(self.name, " drinks some milk.")
        print(self.name, " takes a nap.")
```

Chapter 2: Objects, classes and factories   25

Improving main.py

This is where all that hard work pays off. You are going to order two cats very quickly and play with both. You will probably find the code makes sense without any help this time. Open a new window in IDLE and copy the code from Code Box 2.4. Save it as `main2.py`.

```
Code Box 2.4

import cat2

# create two instances of a cat
romeo = cat2.Cat("Romeo")
juliet = cat2.Cat("Juliet")

# play with Romeo
romeo.speak()
romeo.drink()

# play with Juliet
juliet.speak()
juliet.drink()
```

Run this file and then feel free to play and adjust the code. Have fun!

Designing classes

This section introduces another simple example where you will get to practise what you have learned and you will start to learn how to design a class. You are going to build a lift and a lift operator.

Below is one way to make a class for a lift. There are many properties a lift can have, but in terms of a program there are very few essentials.

The only essential feature of a lift is which floor it is on. Instead of 'essential feature' we could call this a property or characteristic. In programming we call these characteristics **attributes** (or sometimes **parameters**) and we **initialise** them in the constructor.

Class Name
   Lift

Attributes
   current floor

Methods
   get floor
   move to floor

Class design sheet 2.1 A lift class.

Chapter 2: Objects, classes and factories 27

We might also want to know how many passengers it can hold, or its velocity – but this lift is going to be very simple. To plan a lift class we can use a class design sheet. You will find a blank one in the Appendix at the end of this book and also on the companion website – so you can print out your own should you wish. The design work goes into the class design sheet. From this we can build our class.

Two methods are essential: one that finds out what floor the lift is on and another to move the lift to a new floor. Now let's see how this gets turned into code:

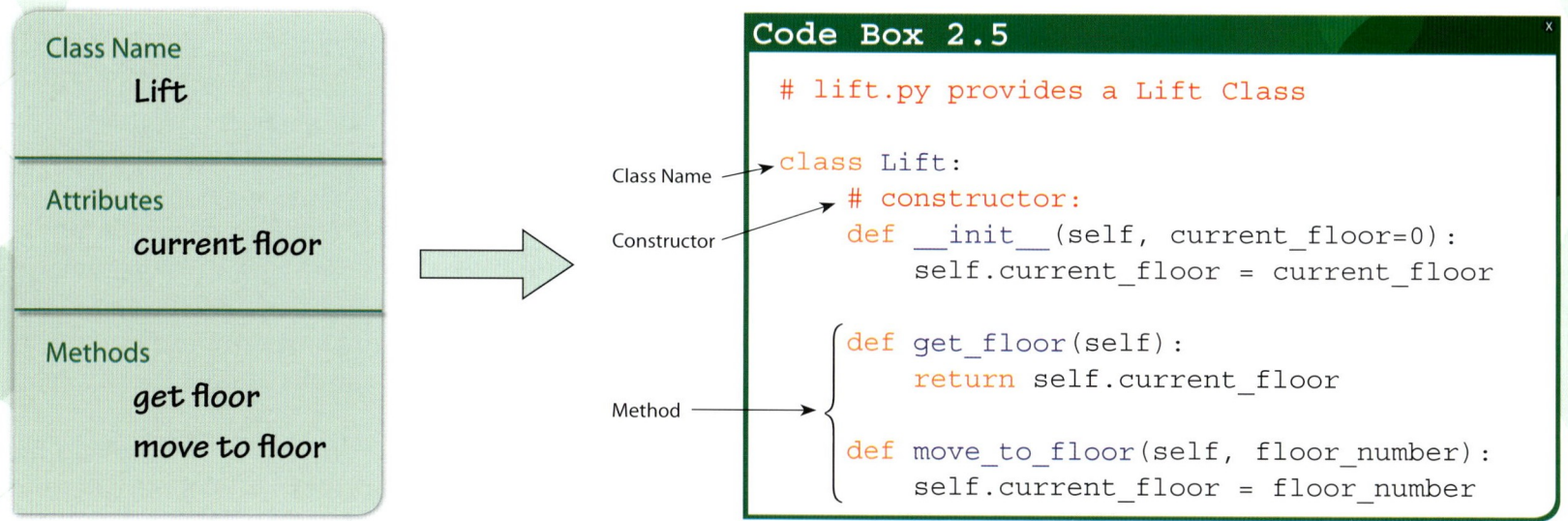

Analysis of Code Box 2.5

There is a **default value** set for the `current_floor` attribute, 0. This can be seen in the constructor method. Now, if we do not pass a `current_floor` argument to this class when it builds a new lift object, the new lift will start on floor 0.

The `return` key word is used in the first method. This means that if we call this method in our lift operator program it will return (give back) the value stored in the `self.current_floor` variable.

The lift operator

`lift_operator.py` has some easy code that plays with the lift. Instead of typing it up you can simply open and run it from the Chapter 2 folder in the source code files you have downloaded from the companion website. The code can be seen on the next page in Code Box 2.6.

Code Box 2.6

```python
# lift_operator.py

import lift

# create a lift object
my_lift = lift.Lift()

# Find out what floor the lift is on
floor = my_lift.get_floor()
print("The lift is on floor", floor)

# move the lift to a new floor
my_lift.move_to_floor(5)

# Find out what floor the lift is on now
floor = my_lift.get_floor()
print("The lift has now moved to floor", floor)
```

Experiment

When creating `my_lift` we did not include a `current_floor` variable so the lift started on floor 0. Try altering this line of code to `my_lift = lift.Lift(3)` and running again. Interesting, huh?

Chapter summary

In this chapter you have learned:

- about classes, objects and how to design them
- how to build your own module
- a little about object-oriented programming – OOP
- what a nuisance `self` can be!

This has been quite an intense chapter. If you are feeling overwhelmed, do not worry as the MyPong project is going to reinforce many of these ideas and you will get the hang of them soon.

If you want some practise, try this easy and relaxing challenge. (Easy and relaxing if you have the code for cat2.py and main2.py in front of you while you complete the challenge!)

Good luck.

A relaxing challenge! That's a new one.

Easy and relaxing challenge

Make a Pet class and save it in a file called `pet.py`.
Make an application called `pet_owner.py` to build and control some pets.
You can choose any pets you like such as hamsters or chinchillas. Alternatively you might prefer tarantulas or piranhas. You will find that you have to be careful with what your pets can do. Piranhas cannot speak or go for walk!

The
MyPong
Project

There have been many versions of Pong made, written in many programming languages. The great thing about Pong is that everyone knows how to play it straight away and it is a great little competitive two-player game. However, building the game is simply a means to an end. The real aim of this project and the book as a whole is to think about how to design bigger applications and how to design the code in a way that it can be re-used in other projects.

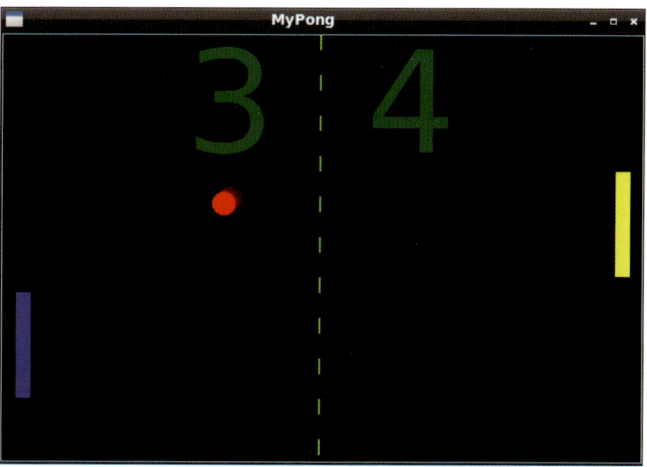

Chapter 3
Creating the Table

It's time to start our project. By the end of this chapter you will have written the code for the first class in our MyPong module. You can download this chapter's files from the companion website. There are two folders: `pong-table-start` and `pong-table-final`. The first folder has Python start files with a skeleton made of comments. The second folder contains the finished files for this chapter in case you cannot get yours to work.

Future chapters follow this pattern. The start files always contain the work you have already done from the previous chapter with additional commenting. This is so that it is never a disaster if you get confused. Another reason for providing all of these backup files is to encourage you to experiment with your code at the end of each chapter without the fear of losing your way. Please though, do try typing rather than just reading the files. You will then be justified in calling MyPong your own when it is complete. You will also have a much better chance of understanding how the code all works.

There is more in this chapter about how to design classes. This theme also continues in the rest of the book.

In this chapter you are going to:

- design a Table class
- learn a bit more about the tkinter module
- build a simple graphical app.

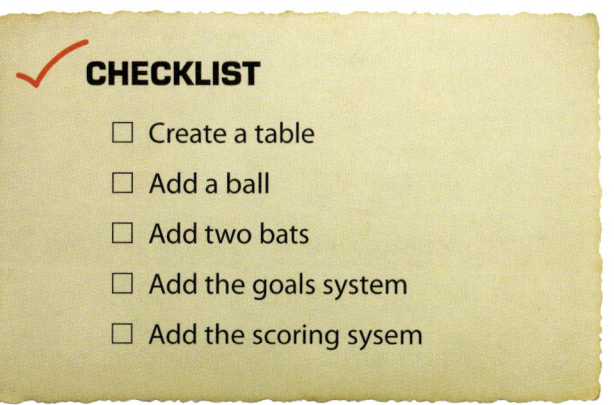

✓ **CHECKLIST**
- ☐ Create a table
- ☐ Add a ball
- ☐ Add two bats
- ☐ Add the goals system
- ☐ Add the scoring sysem

The big plan

Figure 3.1 shows how the final project will look. You will build a group of classes to accomplish this. There will be a Ball class and a Bat class for example. The classes will be built in a way that they could be used in other games. Indeed in the bonus chapter, they will be. There are many games that have balls and bats in them!

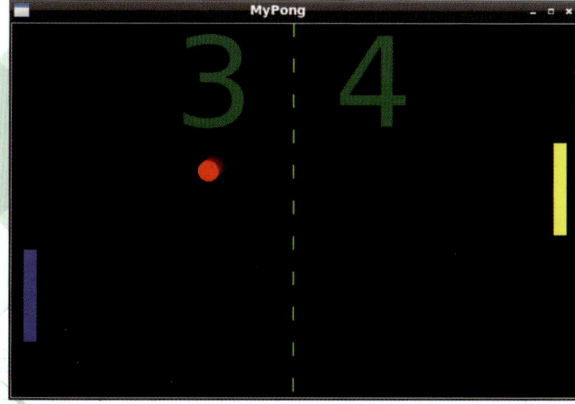

Figure 3.1 The finished MyPong game.

The game is made up of:

- two bats
- a table with a net and a score board
- a ball
- two players.

We now have to decide how to separate this idea into classes by thinking of the objects we require. There are several ways of doing this. Never think there is only one correct answer!

Obviously, we are going to create a Ball class and a Bat class. We will also need a file called `main.py` which will control most things. There has to be a Table class otherwise this chapter's title would make no sense! But what should we do about the net, the rules and the scoring system?

The obvious place for the rules will be in `main.py`. The net is very simple and though we could build a Net class, it seems a lot of effort when all we need to do is draw a dashed line: it can become part of the table. We do not have to program everything at once though. We can wait and see how we feel later. This is the beauty of object-oriented programming in action!

That is enough of a strategy to be able to start designing the first version of our Table class.

The Table class planning page

Here is a planning sketch and a table class design sheet.

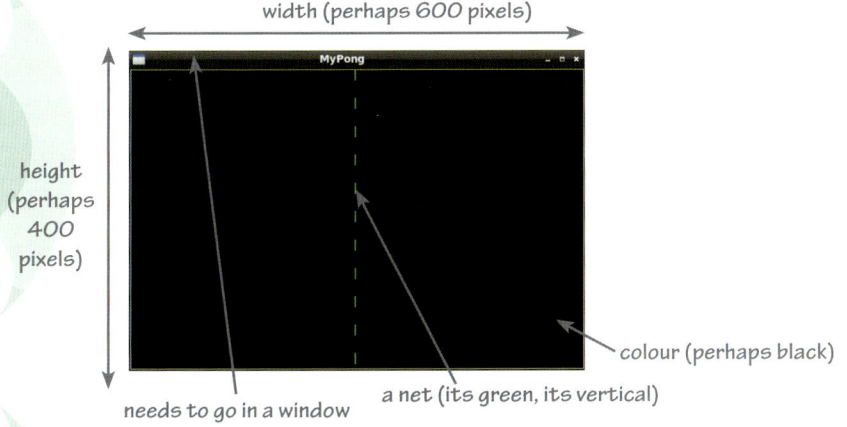

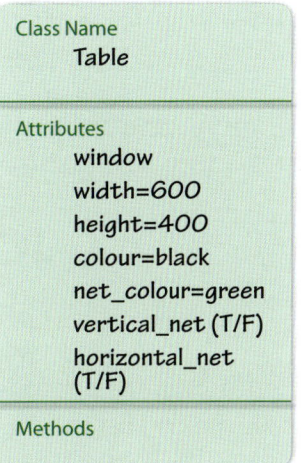

Ah yes, boolean variables: these allow us to clearly see what is True and what is False in the world.

Notes

It will be helpful to supply lots of **default values** such as 600 pixels for width.

The **attributes** are going to go in a lengthy **constructor**.

By having some **boolean variables** for the net position, it will be easy to use this class to build a variety of tables with a net that is either vertical, horizontal or non-existent!

At the moment the table requires no methods.

The tkinter toolkit

An additional group of modules is installed along with Python 3, which provide us with some GUI widgets. These were explored in *Python: Next Steps*.

As we are going to use a lot of the methods from tkinter classes, we can choose to use this line of code:

```
from tkinter import *
```

This means that we can refer to any of tkinter's methods in the rest of our code. We no longer need to precede every method with the name of the module where it can be found: we no longer need to put `tkinter.` at the front of every tkinter method call.

This disadvantage of importing modules like this is we must now avoid using any tkinter method names in our own code.

The Table class constructor

Our constructor needs to be passed an argument for each of the attributes that we want to be selectable when ordering a new object. Then we will assign them to all the `self.variables`, as we have done before.

Open `table.py` from the `pong-table-start` folder. This file can be found in the Chapter 3 folder. Open this with IDLE and add the missing code from Code Box 3.1. Add your code to the file shown in the header bar of the Code Box.

Can you see how this matches the first part of our plan?

Code Box 3.1 — table.py

```python
# This class defines a Table that is a 2D rectangle that is a play area.

from tkinter import *

class Table:
    #### constructor
    def __init__(self, window, colour="black", net_colour="green",
                 width=600, height=400,
                 vertical_net=False, horizontal_net=False):
        self.width = width
        self.height = height
        self.colour = colour
```

I never realised that the British spelt color with a 'u'.

Classes built like this are very much like factories. In `main.py` we will be able to quickly manufacture a table with code such as this:

```
my_table = table.Table(window)
```

Because of all the default values we have supplied in the constructor's `__init__` line, the only argument required will be `window`. The class will make a table object that is just like the one we want, with one exception.

> **? Quick Quiz 3.1**
>
> Look back at the `__init__` line in Code Box 3.1 and the diagram of the required table on the Table class planning page. What will the difference be between the table we get and the one we want?

Building classes in this way means we can build a variety of tables in the future using one line of code. The Table class becomes a very useful little factory (Figure 3.2). Do you want a red table with a horizontal net that is 300 pixels by 300 pixels? Just ask:

```
my_table = table.Table(window, horizontal_net=True, width=300, height=300, colour="red")
```

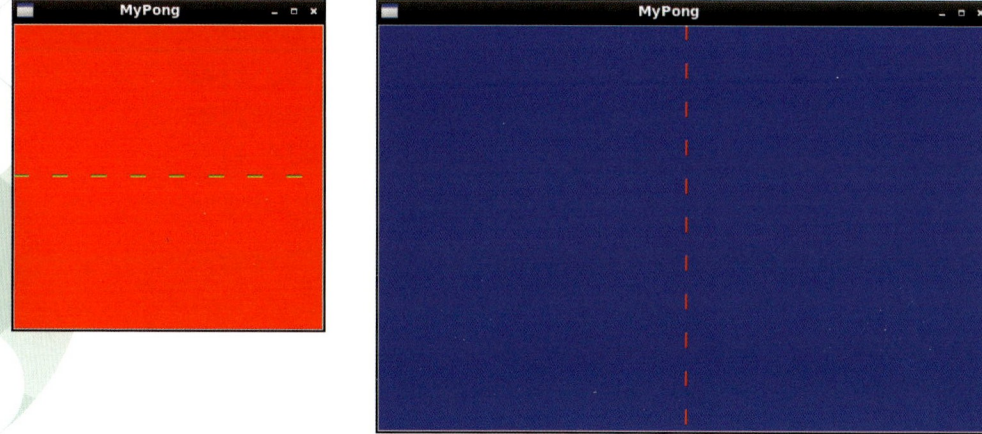

Figure 3.2 Some table objects.

> **? Quick Quiz 3.2**
>
> What would the code be to make a blue table object with a vertical red net, which is 600 pixels wide by 400 pixels tall?

More tkinter tools

The constructor method is not quite finished as we have not told it to actually build the table or the net yet. We will leave the drawing of the window for `main.py` (which will be written very soon). To build our table we have to use some tkinter code which we might have to find by looking up the instructions on the tkinter website. This is quite a large library and you do not need to worry about doing this yourself as it has been done for you. Feel free to look if you are interested. At the time of writing, instructions could be found here:

http://docs.python.org/py3k/library/tk.html

First we are required to make the canvas, which is coded like this:

```
self.canvas = Canvas(window, bg=self.colour, height=self.height, width=self.width)
```

The Canvas class is a tkinter factory that requires the arguments for a window, background colour, height and width – all of which we have variables for in the first part of our constructor.

> ## Delving Deeper
>
> ### When to use self and when it is unnecessary
>
> When we build a class such as a Table class, we need to pass it any attributes it is going to require to build its table objects. For example, the table is going to go in a window object – so we need to pass the window to it as an argument.
>
> If on the other hand we are going to pass the Table class an attribute, such as width, which we might want other classes or files to query (e.g. Table, how wide are you?) then we need to declare it in the constructor as an object variable with `self`. Then, the classes or files could ask the table object how wide it is.

The next thing we have to do is call canvas' `pack()` method. It does not require any arguments:

```
self.canvas.pack()
```

The `pack()` method is required to make our table visible while performing other tasks. Next we can use canvas' `create_line()` method to draw a net. This takes the following form:

```
self.canvas.create_line([top x-coord], [top y-coord], [bottom x-coord],
                       [bottom y-coord], width=2, fill=net_colour, dash=(15, 23))
```

The `width` is in pixels so we want a line that is two pixels thick.

The `fill` is the colour of the line – we have a variable ready for that.

The `dash` attribute takes two numbers – the length of the dash and the spacing, also in pixels.

To understand the coordinates, it helps to know that unlike in maths and science at school, computers often count pixels from the top left corner of the screen or window. This is the case in Python. Look at Figure 3.3 to see how this works.

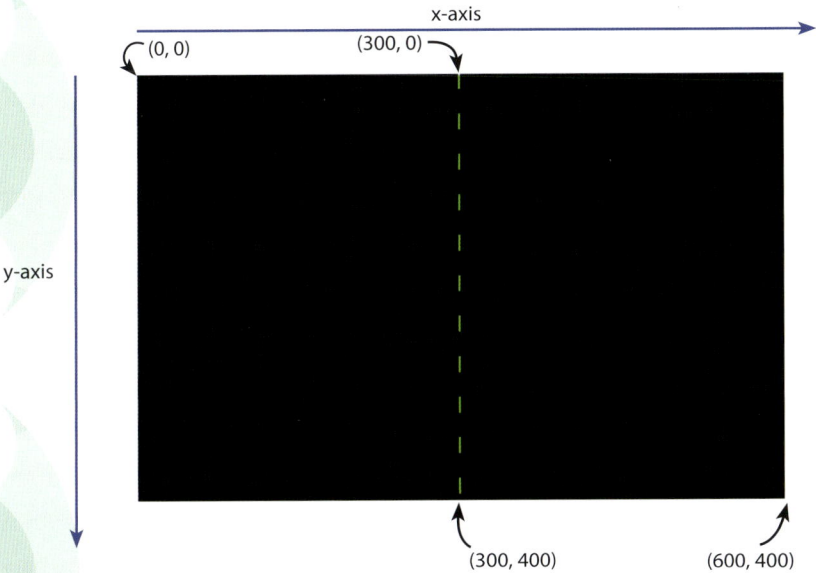

Figure 3.3 Coordinates.

So the call to implement the `create_line()` method, could be written as:

```
self.canvas.create_line(300, 0, 300, 400, width=2, fill=net_colour, dash=(15, 23))
```

This is not, however, a good way of doing it as we are trying to build a Table class. A factory that can only build one type of table is not much use. What if we wanted a longer table? The net would be too far to the left. A taller table would have a net that did not reach the bottom! But we have variables that hold the width and height properties of the table object, so we can calculate the coordinates from these in the method. Then the net will always be in the correct place:

For a vertical net:

`[top x-coord]` becomes `self.width/2`

`[top y-coord]` becomes `0`

`[bottom x-coord]` becomes `self.width/2`

`[bottom y-coord]` becomes `self.height`

For a horizontal net:

`[left x-coord]` becomes `0`

`[left y-coord]` becomes `self.height/2`

`[right x-coord]` becomes `self.width`

`[right y-coord]` becomes `self.height/2`

You can now add the extra code in Code Box 3.2 to your copy of `table.py`. Use the comments in the supplied file to guide you as to where to add the new code.

Code Box 3.2 — `table.py`

```python
        # order a canvas to draw on from the tkinter factory:
        self.canvas = Canvas(window, bg=self.colour, height=self.height, width=self.width)
        self.canvas.pack()

        # add a net to the canvas using a method from the tkinter factory:
        if(vertical_net):
            self.canvas.create_line(self.width/2, 0, self.width/2,
                                    self.height, width=2, fill=net_colour, dash=(15, 23))
        if(horizontal_net):
            self.canvas.create_line(0, self.height/2, self.width,
                                    self.height/2, width=2, fill=net_colour, dash=(15, 23))
```

Warning!

It is easy to make a typing mistake at some stage. Check your code carefully and when you complete it, run the program and see if you can find and correct any problems. If you have any difficulties and start to get frustrated, then the complete file is available from the companion website. After all, coding should be fun. Before using the complete files, please do try to type the code in yourself and think about how each line of code works as you type. You will learn to code better if you do this. (This phrase appears to be in an infinite loop!)

The methods

We will add some methods to this class later. At the moment, all the Table class has to do is be able to create static tables in a variety of shapes!

That finishes the Table class. As classes are factories and not table objects, `table.py` will not do anything if you try to run it. At this stage, we have simply defined a Table class, not manufactured any tables. Even so, please remember to save the file.

main.py

You now have to create the controlling program file called `main.py`. This file will change in future chapters. At the moment it is quite short. The whole file can be seen in Code Box 3.3.

Code Box 3.3 — main.py

```python
# This is the main file for MyPong.

from tkinter import *
import table

# order a window from the tkinter factory
window = Tk()
window.title("MyPong")
```

```python
# order a table from the table factory
my_table = table.Table(window, net_colour="green", vertical_net=True)

# start the animation loop
window.mainloop()
```

A skeleton version of `main.py` is also in your `pong-table-start` folder so you can now open it in IDLE and complete the code from Code Box 3.3.

Analysis of Code Box 3.3

The first two lines of code import the tkinter toolkit and then import our table class file in the normal way.

The next thing that happens in `main.py` is an order is made for a window object, which we call `window`, from the `Tk()` class and we give it a title using the title method. Then a table is ordered from our brand new Table factory which we assign to the variable `my_table`. Finally, to get the whole thing going we call the `window` object's `mainloop()` method. This enters a **loop** where `Tk()` will wait for and react to events. This is needed so that it opens a window containing our table.

Can you see that because we have designed our Table class well, everything we might want to change can be done without opening that class? In other words, we can simply send all our orders and instructions to the various classes in tkinter as well as to those we make ourselves (such as the Table class).

It is so cool how we can now make customised orders for table objects in just one line of code.

Run and test

We are now in a position where we can test our Table class. Both files `table.py` and `main.py` should be complete and in the same folder. In IDLE run the `main.py` file. You should be presented with a table with a net!

If you have any bugs try to sort them out by comparing the colours in your code with those in the Code Boxes in this book. Also, look carefully at the error messages in IDLE. Errors could be in either file – IDLE's messages will tell you where to look. This is called **debugging**. It can be quite tricky sometimes, so if you have tried a few times, please use the two files in the Chapter 3 folder found in the `pong-table-final` folder from the website.

> ## Delving Deeper
>
> ### When to build classes?
>
> You may be wondering when it is best to build classes. Many object-oriented programming (OOP) experts will try and build everything out of classes, including a Main class! However, there are many ways to go about things, OOP is one of them and you have many choices within that. In this book you are being introduced to a selection of OOP techniques which do not harness all of OOP's benefits – or its complexities. The focus of this book is to teach you how to build and interact with classes. We are therefore going to choose a class whenever we want to build an object which we may want to use later in our coding life or when we want many of the same kind of object.
>
> To explain why we want a Table class is easy if you think of classes as factories. Without the net it can be the stage for many games or animations. Later we are going to build a Bat class. We will write it so that it can be a left or right bat. Then we may want to add code so we can have a bottom or top bat. If we were to serve our ball from a bottom bat, it could now be a rocket launcher. If we place a pile of top bats above a bottom bat (Figure 3.4) we could build a MyBreakout game (or should that be called MyBatout?). We would certainly want a lot of bats then, and they could all be quickly built using our Bat class (or Bat factory).

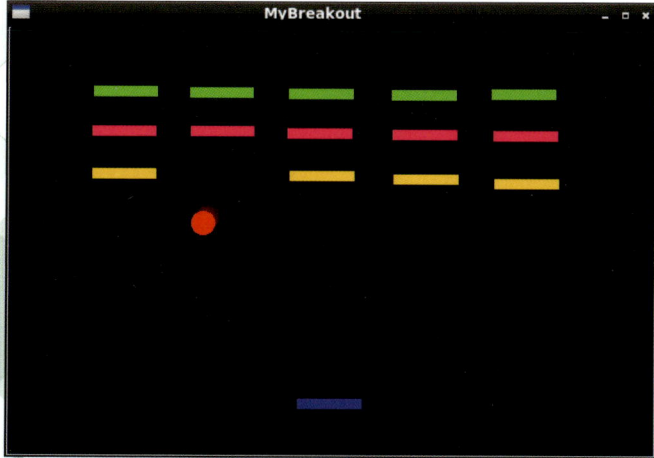

Figure 3.4 Lots of bats.

Chapter summary

In this chapter you have:

- learned more about tkinter
- used your class-building knowledge to build a Table class
- learned a bit more about how classes are like factories
- used tkinter methods to get your computer to put our table in a new window.

Since we have made a factory, the challenges in this chapter are going to involve sending it some orders. If you have downloaded the source code from the companion website, you can now start **hacking** the code without worrying about harming your own files. There are fresh start files ready for each of the remaining chapters so you do not get lost. Challenges 1–4 can all be done in `main.py`.

Challenge 1

Change the title of the window to `My Table Experiment`.

Challenge 2

Create a square table that is blue with a black vertical net.

Challenge 3

Create a table that is black with a horizontal blue net.

Challenge 4

Create a long thin table that is 600 pixels wide and 60 pixels tall.

Challenge 5

Make the table as it was but with a net that is 20 pixels wide. (**Hint**: The line width was **hard coded** (we did not create a variable for it in the constructor) so you will need to adjust the code in the Table class.)

Chapter 4
Making the Ball

By the end of this chapter you will have written the code for the Ball class to go in your MyPong module. We will call it `ball.py`.

There is more in this chapter about how to design classes. There is also a lot of use made of the programming skills that you have already gained. Lots of games use a ball, so we are creating code that is very re-usable.

In this chapter you are going to:

- design a Ball class
- learn how to add the ball to the table
- learn how to animate shapes in tkinter.

Adding a ball

In this chapter we will add a ball to our game (Figure 4.1). First we must design a Ball class and then add it to our table object. The ball is to be a simple circle which moves around the screen bouncing off four walls. We would like to create a class that can be re-used in other games.

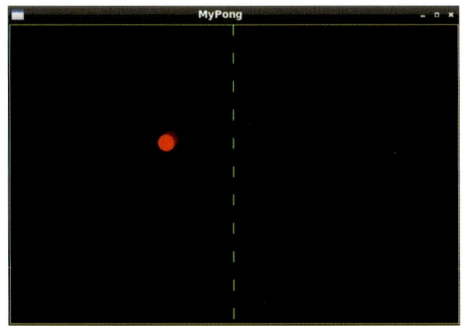

Figure 4.1 The ball in MyPong.

First we need to see how Python draws and positions circles (Figure 4.2):

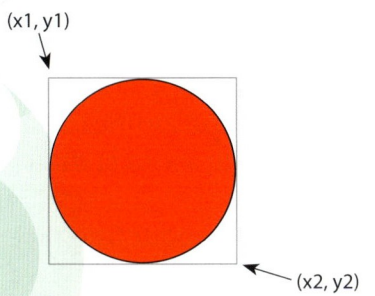

Figure 4.2 Drawing a circle.

The circle is drawn in a square with its position on the table determined by the *x* and *y* coordinates of the top left corner of this square. So to build a circle we provide code like this:

```
self.canvas.create_oval(x1, y1, x2, y2, fill="red")
```

The ball will move and this is controlled by its speed along the *x*-axis and its speed along the *y*-axis. If they are both positive and equal, the ball will move down and to the right, diagonally.

Now let's start our Ball class plan.

Chapter 4: Making the Ball   52

The Ball class planning page

We can get stuck in straight away. We are simply going to build a ball factory so let's get designing:

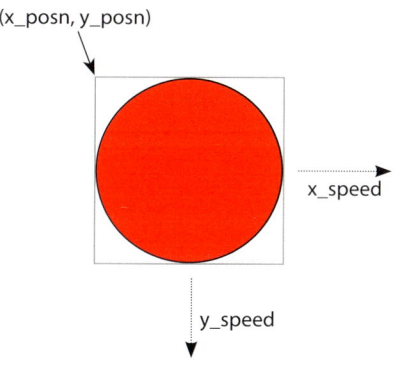
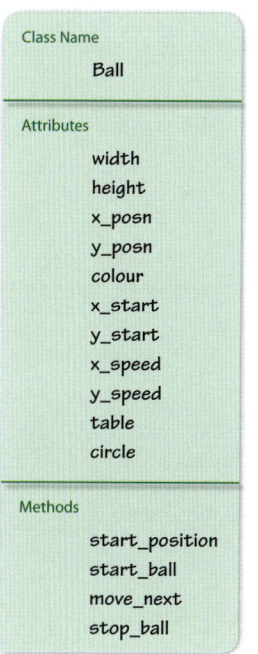

Figure 4.3 The Ball class planning page.

Notes

The first five Ball class attributes should be fairly obvious. Then we add coordinates for where the ball is served from, as well as the horizontal and vertical speed. We also need a circle to be the ball, and our table for the ball to move on.

Let's look at the methods now.

`start_position()`:

This will be a simple method to put the ball back at its start position.

`start_ball()`:

This method will get the ball moving. It sets the required x_speed and y_speed to the ball.

`move_next()`:

Here we will have our most complex method, which will govern how the ball moves. Basically, every 50 milliseconds the ball has to move somewhere else. This method controls where this will be.

`stop_ball()`:

With this simple method we will stop the ball. We set its x_speed and y_speed to zero.

Get typing

You should now open `ball.py` from the `pong-ball-start` within the Chapter 4 folder. Complete this by copying in the missing code from Code Box 4.1. Make sure you think about how the planning sheet gets turned into code as you go. (Are you becoming a faster typist yet?)

Code Box 4.1 — ball.py

```python
import table, random

class Ball:
    #### constructor
    def __init__(self, table, width=14, height=14, colour="red",
                 x_speed=6, y_speed=4, x_start=0, y_start=0):
        self.width = width
        self.height = height
        self.x_posn = x_start
        self.y_posn = y_start
        self.colour = colour

        self.x_start = x_start
        self.y_start = y_start
        self.x_speed = x_speed
        self.y_speed = y_speed
        self.table = table
        self.circle = self.table.draw_oval(self)

    #### methods
    def start_position(self):
        self.x_posn = self.x_start
        self.y_posn = self.y_start
```

(continues on the next page)

```python
def start_ball(self, x_speed, y_speed):
    self.x_speed = -x_speed if random.randint(0,1) else x_speed
    self.y_speed = -y_speed if random.randint(0,1) else y_speed
    self.start_position()

def move_next(self):
    self.x_posn = self.x_posn + self.x_speed
    self.y_posn = self.y_posn + self.y_speed
    # if the ball hits the left wall:
    if(self.x_posn <= 3):
        self.x_posn = 3
        self.x_speed = -self.x_speed
    # if it hits right wall:
    if(self.x_posn >= (self.table.width - (self.width - 3))):
        self.x_posn = (self.table.width - (self.width - 3))
        self.x_speed = -self.x_speed
    # if the ball hits hits the top wall:
    if(self.y_posn <= 3):
        self.y_posn = 3
        self.y_speed = -self.y_speed
    # if it hits bottom wall:
    if(self.y_posn >= (self.table.height - (self.height - 3))):
        self.y_posn = (self.table.height - (self.height - 3))
        self.y_speed = -self.y_speed
```

When I copy code, I always try to predict what is coming next. There are quite a lot of similar methods in the Ball class so I managed to get quite a few correct with this one.

```python
        # finally move the circle:
        x1 = self.x_posn
        x2 = self.x_posn+self.width
        y1 = self.y_posn
        y2 = self.y_posn+self.height
        self.table.move_item(self.circle, x1, y1, x2, y2)

    def stop_ball(self):
        self.x_speed = 0
        self.y_speed = 0
```

Apart from the `move_next()` method there is nothing you should not be able to cope with here. There is a full explanation of the `move_next()` method at the end of the chapter. For now, do not forget to save your work, then we will keep coding.

Getting the ball to move by improving the table

To get the ball to move we need to add a couple of tools to our Table class because this is where the ball has to be drawn. We have already written a Table class in `table.py`. There is another copy of this in the `pong-ball-start` folder for this chapter. This has all the code from before and a blank space for you to add a little bit more.

It is perhaps time to realise why we are using the methods from the tkinter Canvas class. A canvas is a place where we paint. Although our game is representing table tennis and as such we make a Table class, the computer is in fact painting shapes on a rectangle and then re-painting them every 50 milliseconds – hence the idea of a canvas.

The table will eventually have to be able to add circles and rectangles to the canvas so now is the time to give our factory a few new tools. Open `table.py` from the `pong-ball-start` folder. You can study the new `draw_rectangle()` method which calls tkinter's `create_rectangle()` method. This code is also shown in Code Box 4.2.

Code Box 4.2 — table.py

```python
    # extra tool for adding a rectangle to the canvas
    def draw_rectangle(self, rectangle):
        x1 = rectangle.x_posn
        x2 = rectangle.x_posn + rectangle.width
        y1 = rectangle.y_posn
        y2 = rectangle.y_posn + rectangle.height
        c = rectangle.colour
        return self.canvas.create_rectangle(x1, y1, x2, y2, fill=c)
```

Now try to write a `draw_oval()` method using tkinter's `create_oval()` method. Remember that an oval is created inside a box, just like a rectangle. The answer is provided in Code Box 4.3.

Code Box 4.3 — table.py

```python
    # extra tool for adding an oval to the canvas
    def draw_oval(self, oval):
        x1 = oval.x_posn
        x2 = oval.x_posn + oval.width
        y1 = oval.y_posn
        y2 = oval.y_posn + oval.height
        c = oval.colour
        return self.canvas.create_oval(x1, y1, x2, y2, fill=c)
```

This method starts by collecting an oval as an argument. We will be passing it an instance of a ball. To aid readability, we define tkinter's required arguments in terms of our ball object's attributes. Then we draw the ball onto the canvas.

Three more table methods

The table will also need to be able to move balls and rectangles, remove them and change their colour. Several things such as ovals and rectangles use the same method names in tkinter, allowing us to simply supply the table with three generic methods for manipulating items on it. Copy the code from Code Box 4.4 into your `table.py` file to complete the Table class.

Code Box 4.4 — table.py

```python
    # extra tools for manipulating items on the canvas:
    def move_item(self, item, x1, y1, x2, y2):
        self.canvas.coords(item, x1, y1, x2, y2)

    def remove_item(self, item):
        self.canvas.delete(item)

    def change_item_colour(self, item, c):
        self.canvas.itemconfigure(item, fill=c)
```

The `move_item()` method is the most interesting new tool we have supplied to our table factory. It takes six arguments:

`self` – a reference to the current table object built from this class. We do not supply this because it is automatically provided by Python (however, it has to be declared).

`item` – we are going to pass it a reference to the items on our canvas that we want to move. This will work for any item that is contained in a bounding box. In this chapter we pass it the circle that represents our ball.

`x1, y1, x2, y2` – these are the coordinates for the bounding box. `x1` and `y1` are the coordinates for the top left of the box. `x2` and `y2` are the coordinates for the bottom right of the box (Figure 4.3).

There is absolutely no problem improving your classes by supplying new methods when they occur to you. It is just like making a factory more flexible by providing it with new machinery.

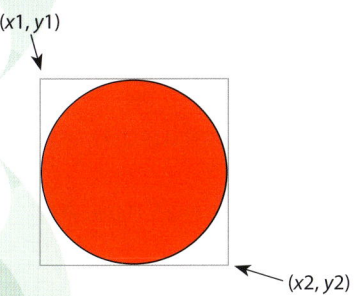

(x1, y1)

(x2, y2)

Figure 4.3 The circle's bounding box.

Adjusting main.py

Now we must adjust `main.py`. This is where we store the rules and run the objects such as the ball. Again there is a starter file from last time with some spaces for you to add the new code. The final file should look like that in Code Box 4.5.

Code Box 4.5 — main.py

```python
from tkinter import *
import table, ball

# initialise global variables
x_velocity = 10
y_velocity = 10

# order a window from the tkinter window factory
window = Tk()
window.title("MyPong")
```

Do not forget to import ball

(continues on the next page)

```python
# order a table from the table factory
my_table = table.Table(window, net_colour="green", vertical_net=True)

# order a ball from the ball factory
my_ball = ball.Ball(table=my_table, x_speed=x_velocity, y_speed=y_velocity,
                    width=24, height=24, colour="red", x_start=288, y_start=188)

#### functions:
def game_flow():
    my_ball.move_next()
    window.after(50, game_flow)

# call the game_flow loop
game_flow()

# start the tkinter loop process
window.mainloop()
```

Analysis of Code Box 4.5

Make sure you add `ball` to the import line – we have a new factory to use.

In the constructor you order a new ball from the Ball class – it is called `my_ball`.

To turn this into a game we will need to add a few functions. Because `main.py` is not a class, it will have functions rather than methods. First, we need a function that animates the ball. `game_flow()` will grow more complex in the next two chapters but for now it calls `my_ball`'s `move_next()` method and then creates an animation loop using the `window.after()` method:

```
window.after(50, game_flow)
```

The first argument selects a 50 millisecond wait, and the second argument gives the function to be called after that wait. The `after()` function has been designed to add an event to the `mainloop()`. In our code, `after()` calls its containing function; therefore, it effectively produces an **infinite loop** where the `my_ball.move_next()` function is called every 50 milliseconds.

Before we call the `mainloop()` method at the end of `main.py`, we need to add one more line of code to call our new function into action: `game_flow()`. Finished!

Delving Deeper

Global or local?

A variable that is created in a function or method is said to be a **local variable**. These variables exist inside the function but are not available to be called or used in the rest of our programs. They can even have the same names as variables in other functions or methods, although this is not a good idea. A **global variable** is often declared at the beginning of our code. We want access to their values at all times. Sometimes we might want to use a global variable inside a method or function. This is fine if we only want to read the value of the

(continues on the next page)

variable. If the method or function needs to change the global variable's value, then it must be re-declared inside the function, with the keyword `global` in front.

If the keyword `global` is omitted, a new local variable with the same name is created. If we do not declare it inside the function at all, then we will get a 'local variable referenced before assignment' error when the function tries to change its value! In other words, the computer does not recognise it as the global variable we intended, and tells us that we are trying to access a non-existent local variable.

Testing and debugging

We are now in a position where we can test our Ball class. First make sure your three files are saved. In IDLE run the `main.py` file. If all is well you should be presented with a table with a net and a red ball that bounces off the walls!

If there are any errors, try to sort them out and take particular notice of which file the error has occurred in. It can be quite tricky sometimes with several files so if you have tried a few times and are not getting anywhere, use the files from the companion website. These can be found in the `pong-ball-final` folder in the Chapter 4 folder. It is a good learning experience to carefully compare your file with the working one. All those days playing spot-the-difference when you were younger will truly pay off now. It is good to notice what errors creep into your code so that you can try to avoid them in the future.

The move_next() method

Earlier it was stated that we would come back and explain the `move_next()` method in `ball.py` – well here is the explanation!

Do feel free to skip to the Challenges section at the end of the chapter if you are feeling a bit worn out. You will still understand enough to mess around with the code and complete the challenges.

To follow this explanation it is best to call up `ball.py` in IDLE so you have the code in front of you. The `move_next()` method has the job of moving the ball to its next position. In `main.py` we call it every 50 milliseconds.

First we add the `x_speed` to the `x_posn` of our ball and then do the same for the `y_posn`. The `x_speed` and `y_speed` are integers. They are the number of pixels to move the ball each 'tick' of the animation. If there are no collisions, this is all that is required to move the ball in a straight line:

```
self.x_posn = self.x_posn + self.x_speed
self.y_posn = self.y_posn + self.y_speed
```

We then need a number of tests to see if the ball has hit any of the walls of our canvas object. The ball's `x_posn` is the top-left coordinate of its bounding box and therefore also the left edge of the circle. So, in the first test we look to see if `x_posn` is less than three pixels from the left wall of the canvas (see the next Delving Deeper to see why we use 3 pixels). If it is, then the `x_speed`'s sign is reversed. A positive `x_speed` sends the ball to the right, while a negative `x_speed` sends the ball to the left. So the speed in this case will have been negative and we are making it positive. That is all that is necessary to bounce the ball.

```
if(self.x_posn <= 3):    # if hits the left wall
    self.x_posn = 3
    self.x_speed = -self.x_speed
```

The move_next() method is not all that bad. If you have the code in front of you while you read the explanation I am sure you'll get it.

The right hand wall is detected and handled in the same way, but detecting the right wall requires us to know the width of the canvas and compare it with 3 pixels less than the right edge of the ball – that is the ball's `x_posn` again plus the ball's width.

The last two `if` statements test for hitting the bottom and top of the canvas and then reverse the `y_speed`.

Finally, we take the results of these tests, compile them into a set of new coordinates and pass them to the `move_item()` method in our table object – found in the Table class:

```
self.table.move_item(self.circle, x1, y1, x2, y2)
```

We have already updated all of the ball's attributes but nothing will appear to happen until we update the position of the circle that represents our ball. This is why we pass `self.circle` rather than just `self` to the `move_item()` method.

Delving Deeper

Why all the threes?

Have you noticed that there are quite a few number threes in this code? Without the threes, the ball does not appear to bounce naturally. Real balls do not turn around as soon as they hit a wall without being squashed. The threes have been added to make this look realistic. The code now does not bounce the ball until it is going to be 3 pixels beyond the wall. Changing the shape of the ball is unnecessarily difficult, but the 3 pixels trick creates the correct illusion.

The 3 pixels trick has been chosen by experimentation, until it looks right. Experimentation sounds so much better than 'trial and error' don't you think?

Chapter summary

In this chapter you have:

- learned more about tkinter
- used your class building knowledge to design and build a Ball class
- learned how accuracy is not as important as the correct illusion.

It is now time to experiment with the ball. So that you do not get confused, shut down IDLE and make a copy of the `pong-ball-final` folder and its contents and call it `pong-ball-challenges`. Now open the `main.py` file from your new folder by double clicking on it. This will open IDLE at the same time. There is no need to fully understand everything to be able to move on. If you can complete some of this chapter's challenges, then you are making great progress.

Challenge 1

Can you make the ball bigger? Does it still bounce well? (Ok, the ball on the right is obviously too big!)

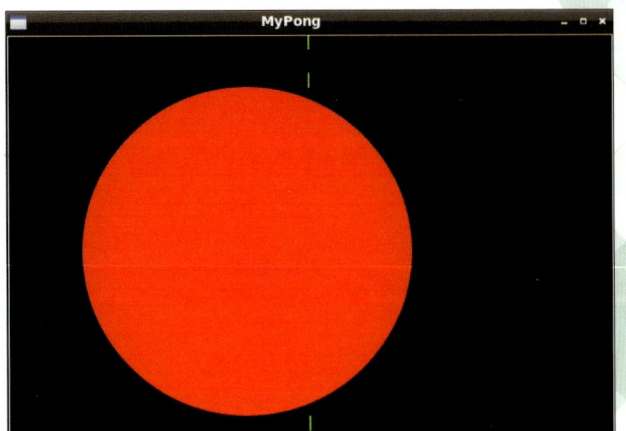

Challenge 2

Find out what happens when you change the `x_speed` and `y_speed`.

Challenge 3

Change the colour of the ball to green. It is best to do this in `main.py`.

Challenge 4

Can you change the shape of the ball so that it looks like a rugby ball? Hint: This can be done in `main.py` when ordering the ball.

Challenge 5

If you want a slightly harder challenge, try to add some gravity to the game. Gravity applies a constant force downward. In terms of code, all you have to do is keep adding a tiny amount of `y_speed` all the time (i.e. at every animation 'tick').

Chapter 5
Building the Bats

By the end of this chapter you will have written the code for the Bat class to go in our MyPong module.

There is more in this chapter about how to design classes and a short section about communication between all of our objects. There is also a lot of use made of the programming skills you have already learned. There are a lot of games that use bats, so again we are creating code that is very re-usable.

The Bat class is our most complicated class.

In this chapter you are going to:

- design a Bat class

- learn how to add bats to the table

- learn how objects communicate with each other.

✓ **CHECKLIST**
- ☑ Create a table
- ☑ Add a ball
- ☐ Add two bats
- ☐ Add the goals system
- ☐ Add the scoring sysem

Adding a bat

In this chapter we will add two bats to our game. First, we must design a Bat class and then use it to manufacture two bats to add to our table object.

The bat is to be a simple rectangle that moves up and down the screen (Figure 5.1). The ball must bounce off our bat in a similar way to the walls. We would like a re-usable class that can be used in other games.

Figure 5.1 The bats in MyPong.

First we need to see how tkinter draws and positions rectangles (Figure 5.2):

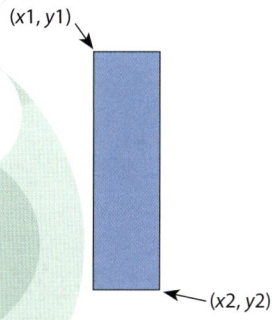

Figure 5.2 Drawing a rectangle.

The rectangle is drawn with its position on the table determined by the $x1$ and $y1$ coordinates of the top left corner. So to build a rectangle we write code like this:

```
self.canvas.create_rectangle(x1, y1, x2, y2, width=10, fill="blue")
```

Note that this is drawn on the canvas and uses the tkinter module. We have prepared for this though and we have already added a draw method to the Table class called `draw_rectangle()`.

The bats will move and this is controlled by their speed along the y-axis. If the speed is positive, the bat will move down vertically.

The `create_rectangle()` method takes a width argument that is the width of the border.

Now let's start our Bat class plan.

The Bat class planning page

On this page we are going to build a bat factory that can produce a left or right bat so let's get designing:

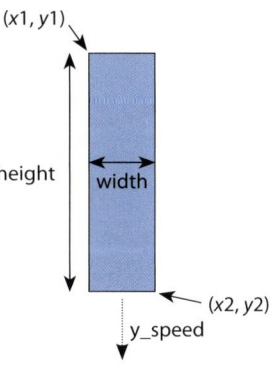

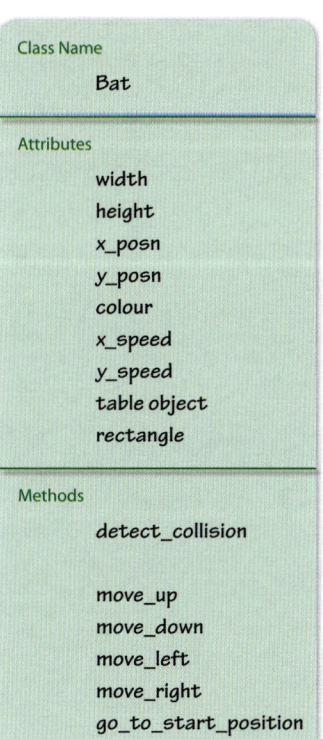

Notes

The first seven Bat-class attributes should be fairly obvious as they are similar to the Ball class (which is also created in a box). We also need a rectangle to be the bat and a table object for the bat to move on. The interesting attributes are the speed attributes:

y_speed

The bat's movement will be attached to a key press. The speed is simply the number of pixels it can jump for each press of the key. So y_speed will be set to a default of 23 pixel jumps (which seems to work well).

```
x_speed
```

This is not required for our game but we want this class to be re-usable in other games – so in it goes. In our game we set x_speed to 0.

In this chapter we will discuss the methods as we require them. The simplest is the `start_position()` method: this will be a simple method to put the ball back at its start position.

Get typing

You should now look inside the Chapter 5 folder and open the `bat.py` file from the `pong-bat-start` folder. There is very little code provided for you this time. You can now add the code from Code Box 5.1 and save it. Again, think carefully about how the planning sheet gets turned into code as you type. You should be able to copy and paste several of the methods and then try to adjust them yourself without looking. This is a great way of learning and reinforcing your new knowledge.

Code Box 5.1 — bat.py

```python
import table

class Bat:
    #### constructor
    def __init__(self, table, width=15, height=100, x_posn=50,
                 y_posn=50, colour="green", x_speed=23, y_speed=23):
        self.width = width
        self.height = height
        self.x_posn = x_posn
```

(continues on the next page)

```python
        self.y_posn = y_posn
        self.colour = colour
        self.x_start = x_posn
        self.y_start = y_posn
        self.x_speed = x_speed
        self.y_speed = y_speed
        self.table = table
        self.rectangle = self.table.draw_rectangle(self)

    #### methods
    def move_up(self, master):
        self.y_posn = self.y_posn - self.y_speed
        if(self.y_posn <= 0):
            self.y_posn = 0
        x1 = self.x_posn
        x2 = self.x_posn+self.width
        y1 = self.y_posn
        y2 = self.y_posn+self.height
        self.table.move_item(self.rectangle, x1, y1, x2, y2)

    def move_down(self, master):
        self.y_posn = self.y_posn + self.y_speed
        far_bottom = self.table.height - self.height
        if(self.y_posn >= far_bottom):
            self.y_posn = far_bottom
        x1 = self.x_posn
        x2 = self.x_posn+self.width
        y1 = self.y_posn
```

```python
        y2 = self.y_posn+self.height
        self.table.move_item(self.rectangle, x1, y1, x2, y2)

    def move_left(self, master):
        self.x_posn = self.x_posn - self.x_speed
        if(self.x_posn <= 0):
            self.x_posn = 0
        x1 = self.x_posn
        x2 = self.x_posn+self.width
        y1 = self.y_posn
        y2 = self.y_posn+self.height
        self.table.move_item(self.rectangle, x1, y1, x2, y2)

    def move_right(self, master):
        self.x_posn = self.x_posn + self.x_speed
        far_right = self.table.width - self.width
        if(self.x_posn >= far_right):
            self.x_posn = far_right
        x1 = self.x_posn
        x2 = self.x_posn+self.width
        y1 = self.y_posn
        y2 = self.y_posn+self.height
        self.table.move_item(self.rectangle, x1, y1, x2, y2)

    def start_position(self):
        self.x_posn = self.x_start
        self.y_posn = self.y_start
```

Getting the bats to move

If you run `main.py` now, you will find that the bats do not appear.

> **❓ Quick Quiz 5.1**
>
> Why do the bats not appear?
> - **A** We have not ordered any bats in main.py.
> - **B** We have not attached their methods to any keyboard input.
> - **C** We have not typed out the code correctly.
> - **D** Table does not know how to draw bats.

So we need to send some orders from `main.py` to our new bat factory for a left and right bat. You should now copy the new code from Code Box 5.2 into `main.py`.

First we order two bats from our new class. Then we attach the movement methods to key presses on the keyboard – you will remember from *Python Basics* that this is pleasingly simple in Python. Here again there is a start file where you will find some spaces for you to add the new code.

Code Box 5.2 — main.py

```python
from tkinter import *
import table, ball, bat

# initialise global variables
x_velocity = 10
y_velocity = 10
```

Do not forget to import the bat class!

```python
# order a window from the tkinter window factory
window = Tk()
window.title("MyPong")

# order a table from the table factory
my_table = table.Table(window, net_colour="green", vertical_net=True)

# order a ball from the ball factory
my_ball = ball.Ball(table=my_table, x_speed=x_velocity, y_speed=y_velocity,
                    width=24, height=24, colour="red", x_start=288, y_start=188)

# order a left and right bat from the bat factory
bat_L = bat.Bat(table=my_table, width=15, height=100, x_posn=20, y_posn=150, colour="blue")
bat_R = bat.Bat(table=my_table, width=15, height=100, x_posn=575, y_posn=150, colour="yellow")

#### functions:
def game_flow():
    # detect if ball has hit the bats:

    my_ball.move_next()
    window.after(50, game_flow)
```

(continues on the next page)

```python
# bind the controls of the bats to keys on the keyboard
window.bind("a", bat_L.move_up)
window.bind("z", bat_L.move_down)
window.bind("<Up>", bat_R.move_up)
window.bind("<Down>", bat_R.move_down)

# call the game_flow loop
game_flow()

# start the tkinter loop process
window.mainloop()
```

Analysis of Code Box 5.2

You should have no problem seeing how the order for the two bats works. The way Python binds methods to key presses is a joy to behold. If you save and run `main.py` now you will see two bats appear that you can move up and down. The ball currently ignores them completely. We still need to add collision detection to the Bat class.

Getting the bats to hit the ball

First let's adjust our `game_flow()` function in `main.py`. With `main.py` still open, adjust the `game_flow()` function so that it matches Code Box 5.3. Please note that the game will no longer work because we have not written the method yet.

Code Box 5.3 — `main.py`

```python
#### functions:
def game_flow():
    # detect if ball has hit the bats:
    bat_L.detect_collision(my_ball)
    bat_R.detect_collision(my_ball)

    my_ball.move_next()
    window.after(50, game_flow)
```

Being clear about classes and objects

In Figure 5.3 you will see a summary of how all the classes are used to build objects and how `main.py` gathers all the objects and runs the game. It is easy to get confused between objects and classes as they often have similar names. Remember that classes all begin with capitals.

It is especially important to be clear when constructing the game in `main.py` because we have to build in the correct order. This is so that when ordering a bat, for example, there is an already built – or **instantiated** – table object. This is not something that is truly easy to get your head around. As you write more and more applications in this way it will become easier. Nevertheless, it is always important to try to understand the relationships between classes and objects so that you can successfully build large applications as you gain more experience.

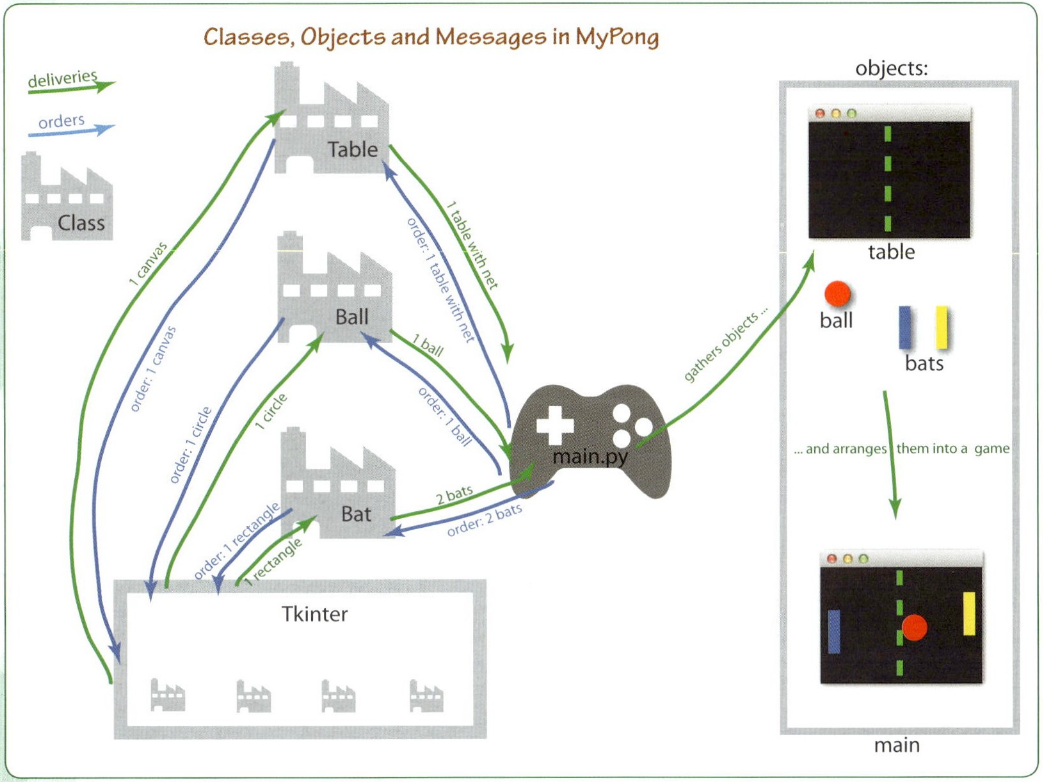

Figure 5.3 Classes, objects and messages.

Detecting if the ball hits the bats

You are now going to add the collision detection function to the bat class in bat.py. When called, a bat object (such as the left bat) will detect if a collision has taken place and can then alter the ball object's (`my_ball`) velocity accordingly.

The final code looks a bit complicated but we will build it a bit at a time. First, re-open the copy of bat.py that you have been working on. Add the new code from Code Box 5.4.

Code Box 5.4 — bat.py

```python
#### methods
def detect_collision(self, ball):
    collision_direction = ""
    collision = False
    feel = 5

    # bat variables:
    top = self.y_posn
    bottom = self.y_posn + self.height
    left = self.x_posn
    right = self.x_posn + self.width
    v_centre = top + (self.height/2)
    h_centre = left + (self.width/2)

    # ball variables:
    top_b = ball.y_posn
    bottom_b = ball.y_posn + ball.height
    left_b = ball.x_posn
    right_b = ball.x_posn + ball.width
    r = (right_b - left_b)/2
    v_centre_b = top_b + r
    h_centre_b = left_b + r
```

(continues on the next page)

```
if((bottom_b > top) and (top_b < bottom) and (right_b > left) and (left_b < right)):
    collision = True
    print("collision")
```

At the beginning of the `detect_collision()` code, all that happens is we define a lot of variables and then detect if there is a collision. These variables are summarised in Figure 5.4.

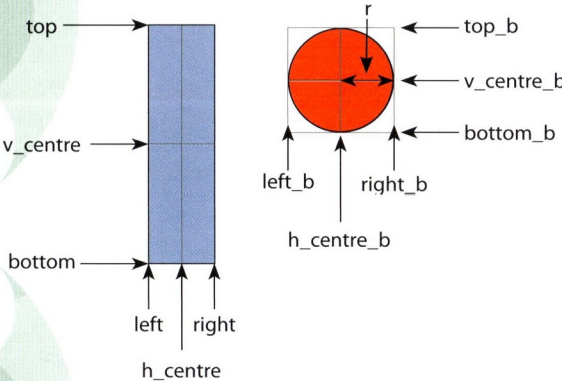

Figure 5.4 Bat and ball variables.

With all the variables added, the `if` clause tests to see if any edge of the ball has entered the space occupied by the bat. If so it sets the variable `collision` to `True` and prints 'collision' to the console. This will be removed later – it is purely for testing purposes. So test it. Save `bat.py` and `main.py` and then run `main.py`. Remember that the ball is still unaffected by this function so passes through the bats but it should send several collision messages to the console as it does. You may have to use the keys to move the bats to get them in the way of the ball.

Delving Deeper

The function design process

The collision detection could be a simple affair if we decided to detect if the ball has reached the leading edge of the two bats. But what if we want to have horizontal bats, or perhaps put them in the centre of the screen and have the ball bounce off all sides? To make the Bat class more useful, we are going to add this full functionality. So with a sketch like the one on page 82 and a coaster and a book to represent a bat and ball colliding, the designer sets about working this out.

All the variables typed here will be used eventually:

`collision_direction`
will store which edge of the bat was collided with (`"N"`, `"S"`, `"E"` or `"W"`).

`collision`
is a boolean variable which will be set to `True` if a collision has been detected.

`feel`
is a constant that we can use to adjust the sensitivity of the angle the ball bounces off the bat later.

Hitting the ball

If all is well, you can delete `print("collision")` from your new function. Now just as in the case of the ball hitting the table wall, all that needs to happen is we reverse the sign of the ball's *x* or *y*-speed. However, we have to know which wall is hit first. This is what the code in Code Box 5.5 does. You can add it now and think about how it works as you type.

Code Box 5.5 — bat.py

```python
if((bottom_b > top) and (top_b < bottom) and (right_b > left) and (left_b < right)):
    collision = True
if(collision):
    if((top_b > top-r) and (bottom_b < bottom+r) and (right_b > right) and (left_b <= right)):
        collision_direction = "E"
        ball.x_speed = abs(ball.x_speed)

    elif((left_b > left-r) and (right_b < right+r) and (bottom_b > bottom) and (top_b <= bottom)):
        collision_direction = "S"
        ball.y_speed = abs(ball.y_speed)

    elif((left_b > left-r) and (right_b < right+r) and (top_b < top) and (bottom_b >= top)):
        collision_direction = "N"
        ball.y_speed = -abs(ball.y_speed)

    elif((top_b > top-r) and (bottom_b < bottom+r) and (left_b < left) and (right_b >= left)):
        collision_direction = "W"
        ball.x_speed = -abs(ball.x_speed)

    else:
        collision_direction = "miss"

    return (collision, collision_direction)
```

Analysis of Code Box 5.5

As well as there being some complicated tests, there are a couple of other things to point out.

`abs()` is a Python function that removes the sign from a number variable. Therefore, both −1.5 and 1.5 become 1.5. It enables us to get the value of the speed without the positive or negative sign.

This function now alters the ball's bounce direction depending on which part of the bat the ball collides with. It does more than this though; it stores which side of the bat the collision occurred at and whether there has been a collision. These two extra bits of information are returned by the function in the last line as a two item **tuple**. We are not going to make use of this currently, but again it makes this a much more useful class: we can also now test for collisions and find out which wall has been hit by selecting which part of the tuple we require, using its **index**:

```
bat_hits_ball=bat_L.detect_collision(my_ball)
print(bat_hits_ball[0])  --> True
```

or

```
bat_hits_ball=bat_L.detect_collision(my_ball)
print(bat_hits_ball[1])  --> N
```

or simply

```
bat_hits_ball=bat_L.detect_collision(my_ball)
print(bat_hits_ball)  --> (True, N)
```

Testing time

If all is well you should have two working bats. The right bat is controlled by the up and down arrows and the left bat is controlled by the a and z keys on your keyboard. They also hit the ball!

In the next chapter, we will add a score board, reset the game, serve the ball and generally finish the project.

Bonus time

This has been a long and complicated chapter – well done if you have followed it all! Before we go on to the Puzzles and Challenges you could give yourself a break! Take a look in the `pong-bat-bonus` folder for this chapter and open `bat.py`. You will see that the `detect_collision()` method has some extra code. What this does is add a 'sweet spot' to the bats: if the ball hits the middle of the bat it hits the ball directly at the opposition. If it does not then it goes off to the side.

All of the code in this book has been tested at the Coding Club. When we first tried to get the ball to collide with the bats I remember distinctly how we had trouble getting the ball to bounce in the way we wanted. It was Ollie who suggested putting in the `return(collision, collision_direction)` code. We were then able to have printouts sent to the console of exactly what was happening. This slows down the ball's movement as well as giving us line-by-line feedback, which proved very helpful in our debugging process. We left the return code in so that if we need to know which face of a bat the ball hits we can easily get the information.

The method can be sent arguments to turn on and off this functionality for either vertical bats or horizontal bats. The new code can be seen in Code Box 5.6 but if you have downloaded the source code there is no need to copy it in – it is supplied for your use.

Code Box 5.6 — `bat.py`

```python
#### methods
    def detect_collision(self, ball, sides_sweet_spot=True, topnbottom_sweet_spot=False):
        collision_direction = ""
        collision = False
        feel = 5
        # bat variables:
        top = self.y_posn
        bottom = self.y_posn + self.height
        left = self.x_posn
        right = self.x_posn + self.width
        v_centre = top + (self.height/2)
        h_centre = left + (self.width/2)
        # ball variables:
        top_b = ball.y_posn
        bottom_b = ball.y_posn + ball.height
        left_b = ball.x_posn
        right_b = ball.x_posn + ball.width
        r = (right_b - left_b)/2
        v_centre_b = top_b + r
        h_centre_b = left_b + r

        if((bottom_b > top) and (top_b < bottom) and (right_b > left) and (left_b < right)):
```

(continues on the next page)

```python
            collision = True
    if(collision):
        if((top_b > top-r) and (bottom_b < bottom+r) and (right_b > right) and (left_b <= right)):
            collision_direction = "E"
            ball.x_speed = abs(ball.x_speed)

        elif((left_b > left-r) and (right_b < right+r) and (bottom_b > bottom) and (top_b <= bottom)):
            collision_direction = "S"
            ball.y_speed = abs(ball.y_speed)

        elif((left_b > left-r) and (right_b < right+r) and (top_b < top) and (bottom_b >= top)):
            collision_direction = "N"
            ball.y_speed = -abs(ball.y_speed)

        elif((top_b > top-r) and (bottom_b < bottom+r) and (left_b < left) and (right_b >= left)):
            collision_direction = "W"
            ball.x_speed = -abs(ball.x_speed)
        else:
            collision_direction = "miss"

        if((sides_sweet_spot == True) and (collision_direction == "W" or collision_direction == "E")):
            # find out how far from the centre of the bat the collision was
            adjustment = (-(v_centre - v_centre_b))/(self.height/2)
            ball.y_speed = feel * adjustment
        if((topnbottom_sweet_spot == True) and (collision_direction == "N" or collision_direction == "S")):
            # find out how far from the centre of the bat the collision was
            adjustment = (-(h_centre - h_centre_b))/(self.width/2)
            ball.x_speed = feel * adjustment

    return (collision, collision_direction)
```

Chapter summary

In this chapter you have:

- learned more about how classes and objects interact
- used your class-building knowledge to design and build a Bat class
- added keyboard control to the `main()` method
- made significant progress towards finishing MyPong.

Now it is time to experiment with the bats. To avoid confusion, shut down IDLE and make a copy of the `pong-bat-final` folder and its contents and call it `pong-bat-working`. Now open the `main.py` file from your new folder by double clicking on it. This will open IDLE at the same time. If you can accomplish some of this chapter's challenges and ideas then you are making great progress.

Challenge 1

Can you make the bats bigger or give them different colours?

Challenge 2

Find out if the bats still behave well with a different sized ball.

Idea 1

Can you spot the difference between the way the bats behave in the game in the final folder versus how they behaved in your game?

Can you see how this was achieved? (**Hint:** look in the `bat.py` file or Code Box 5.5.) It is a matter of taste as to how you want the bats to hit the ball. This new version defines a sweet spot where the ball is hit back perpendicular to the bat if it is hit in the middle. If it is hit on an edge it goes in that direction. Careful positioning of the bat can now be used to control the direction the ball goes. Try changing the arguments when ordering the bats in `main.py` to override the `sides_sweet_spot` argument and see which kind of behaviour you prefer.

I prefer bats without the sweet spots. More 'old school'.

Idea 2

Change the value of the `feel` variable until you are happy with how sensitive the bats are when the sweet spot behaviour is turned on.

I think the sweet spot adds realism.

Idea 3

This is a little bit trickier. Try to change the game so that it is a one-player game with only one bat at the bottom. The object is to stop the ball from hitting the bottom wall. (**Hint:** remember that now you have built robust classes, most tasks can be achieved by ordering the correct kinds of bats and balls from within `main.py`.)

Chapter 6
The rules and scoring

By the end of this chapter you will have completed MyPong and built a useful module for developing other games. In this chapter we will make adjustments to two of our files but we will not make any new classes. There is also more about when to make a new class and when to add methods to your existing classes.

In this chapter you are going to:

- stop the ball bouncing off the left and right walls
- add a scoring system to your game
- finish MyPong!

Scoring a goal

The first job is to make sure that we detect and deal with the ball hitting the left and right walls of our table, because this results in a goal.

So, first we have to detect when the ball hits the left wall. We have already done this in the Ball class:

```
if(self.x_posn <= 3):
    # further code goes here
```

The Ball class is not where we want to change this behaviour as it will become less useful for other games. Instead we will detect the collision in main.py and handle it in a new way. This is because this is a specific rule for this game.

Let's see how hard it is to write it out again in main.py:

```
if(my_ball.x_posn <= 3):
    # further code goes here
```

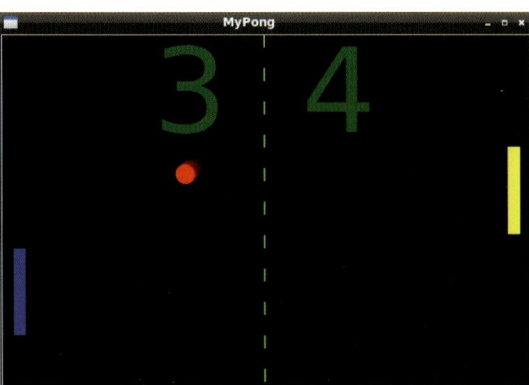

Delving Deeper

The need for 3 pixels again

The logical thing to do would be to test to see if the left side of the ball reaches 0 – this will often not be the case because the ball is really an animation of a circle jumping from one position to the next. So instead, we test if it is within 3 pixels.

Now to add the code to deal with the ball hitting the left wall. In the Chapter 6 folder, open `main.py` in the `pong-score-start` folder. Amend the code in the `move_next()` method in line with the code supplied in Code Box 6.1.

Code Box 6.1 — main.py

```python
    # detect if ball has hit the left wall:
    if(my_ball.x_posn <= 3):
        my_ball.stop_ball()
        my_ball.start_position()
        bat_L.start_position()
        bat_R.start_position()
        my_table.move_item(bat_L.rectangle, 20, 150, 35, 250)
        my_table.move_item(bat_R.rectangle, 575, 150, 590, 250)
```

Analysis of Code Box 6.1

By now you can hopefully understand most of this code. First, we stop the ball and reset its position. Then we reset the bats to their starting positions. Finally, we need to call the table's `move_item()` method twice to move the two rectangles that represent our bats to their starting positions. We do not need to move the circle because the ball looks after this in its `move_next()` method. Later in this chapter we will add a scoring system.

If you run `main.py` it should start OK with the ball in the centre of the canvas. If the ball hits the left wall it will go back to the centre and the bats return to their start positions. The bats are still moveable. The ball is now stuck.

Now copy and paste the code for detecting the left wall to the space in `main.py` waiting for the detection of the right wall. Then see if you can adjust it so that the ball goes back to the centre if it hits either wall. If you get stuck, look at Code Box 6.2

Code Box 6.2 — main.py

```python
# detect if ball has hit the right wall:
if(my_ball.x_posn + my_ball.width >= my_table.width - 3):
    my_ball.stop_ball()
    my_ball.start_position()
    bat_L.start_position()
    bat_R.start_position()
    my_table.move_item(bat_L.rectangle, 20, 150, 35, 250)
    my_table.move_item(bat_R.rectangle, 575, 150, 590, 250)
```

Adding the ability to serve

It is of course no good if the ball just stops and resets itself and the game ends – so we need to be able to serve. To do this, we must add a `restart()` function to `main.py`. Add the code from Code Box 6.3 to your `main.py` file in the place indicated by the comments.

Code Box 6.3 — main.py

```python
# bind restart to spacebar
window.bind("<space>", restart_game)
```

The first part of the `restart_game()` function has been added for you. It is below the `game_flow()` function. The code is shown in Code Box 6.4. The new code is added just above the keyboard bindings:

Code Box 6.4 — main.py

```python
# add restart_game function here:
def restart_game(master):
    my_ball.start_ball(x_speed=x_velocity, y_speed=0)
```

There are a few things to note here. Tkinter expects an extra argument in this function, so we are required to add `master`. This is beyond the scope of this book but please note that it is necessary. In the ball object's `start_ball()` method, we have supplied `y_speed=0` as an argument because we do not want the ball's default `y_speed`. This means the serve will now be horizontal instead of diagonal.

> **Experiment**
>
> Save and run `main.py` to see how the app works so far. Click in the game window with your mouse to gain focus and then try pressing the space bar a few times to see how `restart_game()` works. You can also try changing the value of `y_speed` and see what effect that has – you might prefer it.

The first serve

Now to sort out the first serve. At the moment, the game just starts before we are ready, so we will add a new global boolean variable to store whether we are on the first serve or not.

In the space provided, near the top of `main.py`, add the code from Code Box 6.5. While you are doing this, you can also add the variables to hold the scores.

Code Box 6.5 — `main.py`

```python
# initialise global variables
x_velocity = 10
y_velocity = 0
score_left = 0
score_right = 0
first_serve = True
```

Now we just need to adjust the `game_flow()` so that it adds an `if` clause and waits for the first serve.

Add the code from Code Box 6.6. You are saving regularly aren't you? As this function can change our new global variables, we must declare them again inside the function.

```
#### functions:
def game_flow():
    global first_serve
    global score_left
    global score_right
    # wait for first serve:
    if(first_serve == True):
        my_ball.stop_ball()
        first_serve = False
```
Code Box 6.6 — main.py

We now know when the first serve has taken place, so we know when to start scoring. All that is left to add is a scoreboard.

The scoreboard

When we planned this game at the beginning of Chapter 3, we were not sure where we were going to put the scoreboard. It now seems a little more obvious. We could set up another scoring class but this seems unnecessary when almost all games have their own scoring system and it is really part of the rules. In MyPong we score by simply adding one

CHECKLIST
- ☑ Create a table
- ☑ Add a ball
- ☑ Add two bats
- ☑ Add the goals system
- ☐ Add the scoring sysem

to each player's current score each time they score a goal. Hence the scoring rules can go in `main.py`.

What about displaying the score? There are many ways of doing this. One that is often used successfully is simply to write the score on the canvas. This is what we shall do. As such, it makes sense to improve our Table class and give it the ability to not only draw a ball and bats on it but to be able to draw the score as well.

We are now going to initialise two more variables in the constructor. We will refer to the players as the left player and the right player as these are the places where their bats will be, the score on the screen will be and the control keys on the keyboard will be. First we add variables to hold our chosen font and a canvas text widget to the constructor, where there is a space waiting. Open `table.py` from the `pong-score-start` folder and add the code from Code Box 6.7 where required.

Code Box 6.7

```
# add scoreboard:
font = ("monaco", 72)
self.scoreboard = self.canvas.create_text(300, 65, font=font, fill="darkgreen")
```

With the constructor finished, we need to finish off our Table class once and for all by adding a method to draw the scores to the canvas. You can add this to the bottom of the Table class by copying in the code from Code Box 6.8.

Code Box 6.8 — table.py

```python
# extra tool for adding the score to the canvas:
def draw_score(self, left, right):
    scores = str(right) + "  " + str(left)
    self.canvas.itemconfigure(self.scoreboard, text=scores)
```

Now that you are an experienced coder, you should find that you can understand quite a lot here. Remember that our table object is built with a canvas ordered from the tkinter library and as such has the canvas methods available to it. The `itemconfigure()` method has been used before but now you can see how it works with text. The default values place the text at the top of the canvas and centre it, which is ideal. We simply have to pass it a string to use for the scoreboard. However, the `itemconfigure()` method expects strings not integers so we change the integers into strings with the Python `str()` method and build these into one string first.

Delving Deeper

Casting and concatenating

You know that variables can keep references to text and numbers etc. These are called **data-types** in computer science. The ones you are most familiar with are strings and integers, but there are several others.

In many languages you must declare what type of data a variable is referring to when it is made. This is not necessary in Python; however, it is not possible to suddenly use an integer as a string. It must be changed by **casting**.

We cast integers into strings with the `str()` function. Numbers that are stored as strings can be converted into integers with the `int()` function.

When we join strings together to make one string, this is called **concatenating**, as we have done with `scores`.

Final steps

`table.py` is complete. Now save it and re-open `main.py`. There is nothing much to do here except add the scoring functionality (the rules) in three places:

- when the game is started we want to set the scores to zero
- when the ball hits the left wall we want to add one to the right player's score
- when the ball hits the right wall we want to add one to the left player's score.

Copy in the new code indicated in Code Box 6.9, which shows the complete code for `main.py`. If all goes well you should have a fully functioning game – with a scoreboard.

Code Box 6.9 — main.py

```python
from tkinter import *
import table, ball, bat

# initialise global variables
x_velocity = 10
y_velocity = 0
score_left = 0
score_right = 0
first_serve = True
```

```python
# order a window from the tkinter window factory
window = Tk()
window.title("MyPong")

# order a table from the table factory
my_table = table.Table(window, net_colour="green", vertical_net=True)

# order a ball from the ball factory
my_ball = ball.Ball(table=my_table, x_speed=x_velocity, y_speed=y_velocity,
                    width=24, height=24, colour="red", x_start=288, y_start=188)

# order a left and right bat from the bat factory
bat_L = bat.Bat(table=my_table, width=15, height=100, x_posn=20, y_posn=150, colour="blue")
bat_R = bat.Bat(table=my_table, width=15, height=100, x_posn=575, y_posn=150, colour="yellow")

#### functions:
def game_flow():
    global first_serve
    global score_left
    global score_right
    # wait for first serve:
    if(first_serve == True):
        my_ball.stop_ball()
        first_serve = False
```

(continues on the next page)

```
# detect if ball has hit the bats:
bat_L.detect_collision(my_ball)
bat_R.detect_collision(my_ball)

# detect if the ball has hit the left wall:
if(my_ball.x_posn <= 3):
    my_ball.stop_ball()
    my_ball.start_position()
    bat_L.start_position()
    bat_R.start_position()
    my_table.move_item(bat_L.rectangle, 20, 150, 35, 250)
    my_table.move_item(bat_R.rectangle, 575, 150, 590, 250)
    score_left = score_left + 1
    if(score_left >= 10):
        score_left = "W"
        score_right = "L"
    first_serve = True
    my_table.draw_score(score_left, score_right)

# detect if the ball has hit the right wall:
if(my_ball.x_posn + my_ball.width >= my_table.width - 3):
    my_ball.stop_ball()
    my_ball.start_position()
    bat_L.start_position()
    bat_R.start_position()
    my_table.move_item(bat_L.rectangle, 20, 150, 35, 250)
    my_table.move_item(bat_R.rectangle, 575, 150, 590, 250)
```

```python
        score_right = score_right + 1
        if(score_right >= 10):
            score_right = "W"
            score_left = "L"
        first_serve=True
        my_table.draw_score(score_left, score_right)

    my_ball.move_next()
    window.after(50, game_flow)

#add restart_game function here
def restart_game(master):
    global score_left
    global score_right
    my_ball.start_ball(x_speed=x_velocity, y_speed=0)
    if(score_left == "W" or score_left == "L"):
        score_left = 0
        score_right = 0
    my_table.draw_score(score_left, score_right)

# bind the controls of the bats to keys on the keyboard
window.bind("a", bat_L.move_up)
window.bind("z", bat_L.move_down)
window.bind("<Up>", bat_R.move_up)
window.bind("<Down>", bat_R.move_down)
```

(continues on the next page)

```python
# bind restart to the spacebar
window.bind("<space>", restart_game)

# call the game_flow loop
game_flow()

# start the tkinter loop process
window.mainloop()
```

Chapter summary

In this chapter you have:

- created a goal detection system
- added a scoring system to your game and a scoreboard
- learned that there are many ways of achieving the same result and that they do not always have to involve building a new class
- finished MyPong!

CHECKLIST
- ☑ Create a table
- ☑ Add a ball
- ☑ Add two bats
- ☑ Add the goals system
- ☑ Add the scoring sysem

It can be fun to work hard and learn things; however, it is also very rewarding to finish a project. You can of course now play with your creation. Go ahead and challenge someone! This is the best way to find out what you like and dislike about the game design. This process has a name – game testing. The great thing is, you can now customise it and get it to perform exactly the way you like.

Instead of challenges, there are just some ideas that you may wish to consider when customising your game. Congratulations on getting this far, have fun and keep coding!

Idea 1

You will probably want to speed the ball up a bit as it is set quite slow for testing purposes. This can be done in the `main.py` constructor.

Idea 2

Try moving the bats nearer the middle to increase the tension.

Idea 3

Try changing the size of the bats and their colour.

Idea 4

Try adding keyboard control so the bats can move towards the net and back. You could limit them to their side of the board, or if you enjoy mayhem – leave them as they are!

Bonus chapter
Two more games

This chapter demonstrates the benefits of building classes well. It has taken four chapters to build MyPong. In this chapter we will build a quick breakout game and an invaders game – all without altering anything except `main.py`. Again, you can work on the start files provided on the website.

Each book in the *Coding Club* series tries to supply at least one bonus project. The purpose of these is to provide some code that does not have any explanations. It is an important skill for coders to develop – to be able to look at other people's code and try to work out what is going on. Although you might not understand everything, you are sure to learn something!

In this chapter you are going to:

- see how useful **lists** are for storing items in games and to keep track of them

- see how to add many bricks at once using a loop

- see how flexible your Ball, Bat and Table classes are

- finish the book with two new games that can be further customised to make them more polished.

MyBreakout

The first game is a very simple game where the goal is to use a ball to clear a load of bricks by hitting them with the ball (Figure 7.1). The player has a bat to rebound the ball and the ball must not get past it to the bottom of the window.

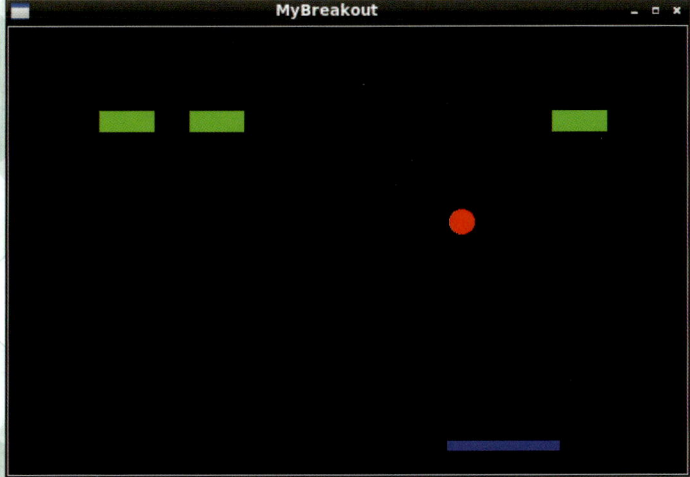

Figure 7.1 MyBreakout.

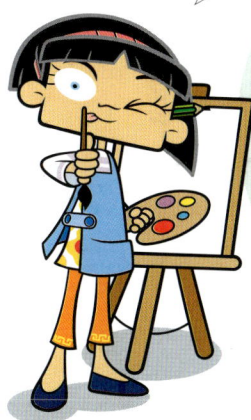

It is probably time to start using the language of professional coders. We should say: we make a bat instance from the Bat class which is placed at the bottom of our table object. We also make a ball instance from the Ball class and then instantiate several bricks from the Bat class.

To build the game, we order a bat from the Bat factory and it is placed at the bottom of the screen. We order a ball from the ball factory. Everything is placed on a table which we order from the Table factory.

The bricks to get rid of are simply more bats from the Bat factory. We do not add any movement or control to these. Instead, after detecting a collision we destroy them. The code is not too difficult. It can be found in Code Box 7.1.

Code Box 7.1

```python
from tkinter import *
import table, ball, bat, random


window = Tk()
window.title("MyBreakout")
my_table = table.Table(window)

# initialise global variables
x_velocity = 4
y_velocity = 10
first_serve = True

# order a ball from the ball class
my_ball = ball.Ball(table = my_table, x_speed=x_velocity, y_speed=y_velocity,
            width=24, height=24, colour="red", x_start=288, y_start=188)

# order a bat from the bat class
bat_B = bat.Bat(table = my_table, width=100, height=10,
            x_posn=250, y_posn=370, colour="blue")

# order further bats from the bat class but call them bricks
bricks = []
b=1
```

```python
while b < 7:
    i=80
    bricks.append(bat.Bat(table = my_table, width=50, height=20,
                          x_posn=(b*i), y_posn=75, colour="green"))
    b = b+1

#### functions:
def game_flow():
    global first_serve
    # wait for first serve:
    if(first_serve==True):
        my_ball.stop_ball()
        first_serve = False

    # detect if ball has hit the bat:
    bat_B.detect_collision(my_ball, sides_sweet_spot=False, topnbottom_sweet_spot=True)

    # detect if ball has hit the bricks:
    for b in bricks:
        if(b.detect_collision(my_ball, sides_sweet_spot=False) != None):
            my_table.remove_item(b.rectangle)
            bricks.remove(b)
        if(len(bricks) == 0):
            my_ball.stop_ball()
            my_ball.start_position()
            my_table.draw_score("", "  YOU WIN!")
```

(continues on the next page)

```python
    # detect if ball hit the bottom wall:
    if(my_ball.y_posn >= my_table.height - my_ball.height):
        my_ball.stop_ball()
        my_ball.start_position()
        first_serve = True
        my_table.draw_score("", "   WHOOPS!")

    my_ball.move_next()
    window.after(50, game_flow)

def restart_game(master):
    my_ball.start_ball(x_speed=x_velocity, y_speed=y_velocity)
    my_table.draw_score("", "")

# bind the controls of the bat to keys on the keyboard
window.bind("<Left>", bat_B.move_left)
window.bind("<Right>", bat_B.move_right)

# bind restart to spacebar
window.bind("<space>", restart_game)

game_flow()
window.mainloop()
```

MyInvaders

The second game is a little more complex and involves defeating an invading fleet of aliens that are intent on landing on Earth (Figure 7.2). This is done by shooting them out of the sky with a tank that can shoot missiles vertically. The tank is a bat, like in MyBreakout. The missile is an oval shaped ball. The invaders are more bat instances, which can move this time.

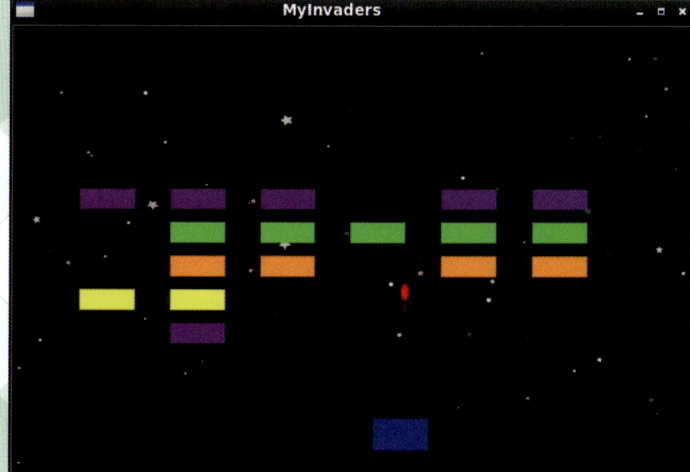

Figure 7.2 MyInvaders.

There are little things to watch out for, such as that the ball is served from the tank each time and hidden when not required. Although this is more complicated than the last game, it takes full advantage of the classes we have built so carefully. Neither game alters them at all.

Enough about the game. Start it up and play. Then have a look at the code and have fun hacking it. The full source code can be seen in Code Box 7.2.

Code Box 7.2

```python
from tkinter import *
import table, ball, bat, random

window = Tk()
window.title("MyInvaders")
my_table = table.Table(window)

# add background image
starry_night_image = PhotoImage(file = "stars.gif")
my_table.canvas.create_image(0, 0, anchor=NW, image = starry_night_image, tags="bg_img")

# move the image to bottom of image stack (so the scoreboard can be seen above the background)
# by moving any canvas objects tagged as "bg_img" to the back using the lower() method
my_table.canvas.lower("bg_img")

# initialise global variables
x_velocity = 0
y_velocity = -10
first_serve = True
direction = "right"

# order a missile from the ball class
my_ball = ball.Ball(table=my_table, x_speed=x_velocity, y_speed=y_velocity,
                    height=15, width=8, colour="black")
```

```python
# order a defender from the bat class
bat_B = bat.Bat(table=my_table, width=50, height=30, x_posn=250, y_posn=350, colour="blue")

# order invaders from the bat class and start them moving to the right
invaders = []
rows=0
gap=30
colour = ("green", "orange", "yellow", "purple")
while rows < 5:
    n=1
    while n < 7:
        i=80
        invader = bat.Bat(table=my_table, width=50, height=20, x_speed=3, y_speed=15,
                    x_posn=(n*i), y_posn=25+(rows*gap), colour=colour[(rows-1) %4])
        invaders.append(invader)
        n = n+1
    rows = rows+1

#### Functions:
def game_flow():
    global first_serve
    global direction
    game_over = False
    # wait for first serve:
    if(first_serve == True):
        my_ball.stop_ball()
        first_serve = False
```

(continues on the next page)

```python
# detect if missile has hit an invader:
for b in invaders:
    if(b.detect_collision(my_ball, sides_sweet_spot=False) != None):
        my_table.remove_item(b.rectangle)
        invaders.remove(b)
        hide_missile()

    if(len(invaders) == 0):
        my_table.remove_item(my_ball.circle)
        my_table.canvas.itemconfigure(my_table.scoreboard, text="YOU WIN")

# detect if missile hit the top wall:
if(my_ball.y_posn <= 3):
    hide_missile()
    first_serve=True

my_ball.move_next()

# handle movement of invaders
directionChange = False;
for b in invaders:
    directionChange = directionChange or move_brick_next(b, direction)
    game_over = detect_game_over(b, bat_B.y_posn)
if(game_over):
    my_ball.stop_ball()
```

```python
        for b in invaders:
            b.x_speed=0
            b.y_speed=0
        my_table.canvas.itemconfigure(my_table.scoreboard, text="GAME OVER")
    if(directionChange):
        for b in invaders:
            b.move_down(b)
        if(direction == "right"):
            direction = "left"
        else:
            direction = "right"
    window.after(50, game_flow)

def restart_game(master):
    first_serve = False
    my_ball.start_ball(0,0)
    my_ball.x_speed=x_velocity
    my_ball.y_speed=y_velocity
    my_table.change_item_colour(my_ball.circle, "red")
    my_ball.x_posn = (bat_B.x_posn + bat_B.width/2)
    my_ball.y_posn = bat_B.y_posn

# Moves invaders to left or right and looks to see if they should be moved down
# returns true if direction must change
def move_brick_next(brick, direction):
    if(direction == "left"):
        brick.move_left(brick)
```

(continues on the next page)

```python
            if(brick.x_posn < 10):    # if the brick reaches the left wall
                return True
            else:
                return False
        else:
            brick.move_right(brick)
            if((brick.x_posn + brick.width) > my_table.width-10):    # if the brick reaches the right wall
                return True
            else:
                return False

# detect if invaders reach the bottom
def detect_game_over(invader, bottom):
    if((invader.y_posn + invader.height) > bottom):
        return True
    else:
        return False

# hide missile
def hide_missile():
    my_ball.stop_ball()
    my_ball.x_posn=0
    my_ball.y_posn=my_table.height-my_ball.height
    my_table.change_item_colour(my_ball.circle, "black")
```

```
# bind the controls of the bat to keys on the keyboard
window.bind("<Left>", bat_B.move_left)
window.bind("<Right>", bat_B.move_right)

# bind restart to spacebar
window.bind("<space>", restart_game)

game_flow()
window.mainloop()
```

Bonus chapter summary

In this chapter you have:

- seen how useful lists are to store items in games and to keep track of them
- seen how to add many bricks at once using a loop
- seen how flexible your Ball, Bat and Table classes are
- played with two new games.

Here are some ideas to use with these new projects:

Idea 1

Add more bricks to MyBreakout.

Idea 2

Play around with the different ways you have learned about how to rebound the ball from the MyBreakout bat.

Idea 3

Add vertical movement to the bat in MyBreakout.

Idea 4

In both games, there is no reason why you cannot try to make the bricks or invaders shoot back!

Idea 5

In MyInvaders make the invaders move faster as time goes on.

Idea 6

Enable multiple missile launching capability in MyInvaders. Currently you can only fire a new ball when the previous one is removed from the screen. This new idea might make the game too easy.

Idea 7

Add a 'number of lives' left, scoring system to either game and perhaps have new levels instead of winning.

Idea 8

Look for other games that use balls and bats (or bricks) and try to build one, or of course, just design your own unique game. Nobody seems to have created 'keepy-uppy' – this would involve gravity and perhaps some random winds!

These are great. I can think of loads of ideas that really would make these into cool games.

Taking things further

When you have finished this book your adventure really begins! You might want to develop your own projects now in Python. Should you be interested, you are now in a good position to start a new language. You will find that all you need to do is look up the syntax used in the new language to indicate loops or classes etc. You will find there are a lot of similarities in, for example, *PHP*, *Java* and the *C* family of languages. Alternatively, you might want to delve into some other tools and libraries that add functionality to Python. Here are some starting points:

The Python stuff

Coding Club books

This is the first Level 3 book in the series but you may still find things to interest you in any of the other project books at lower levels.

http://www.codingclub.co.uk

PyGame

This popular library currently works best using Python 2 rather than 3 but there is not too much difference. The library makes extensive use of classes in its game implementation.

http://www.pygame.org/

PiFace

If you have a Raspberry Pi you may want to try your hand at physical computing. One way of doing this is to purchase a PiFace from Manchester University which can be programmed directly in Python. It will enable you to use your computer to control all sorts of things by interfacing with a scalextric set or a talking chicken, for instance.

http://pi.cs.man.ac.uk/

Non-Python stuff

Arduino

This is an alternative to the PiFace for physical computing. It works with any type of computer rather than just a Raspberry Pi. The language used is C but you will find that to sense and control uses far less complicated code than we have been using in this book, so it will not take you very long to get used to it.

http://www.arduino.cc

GameMaker

This has been popular in some schools for a number of years. It uses a drag-and-drop system for building games. After a while though, this becomes limiting. At this point you can add your own code or download others. Now you will be in a position to understand the code and design your own.

http://www.yoyogames.com/

Greenfoot

If you really love the idea of building code in an OOP way, there is no better way of exploring this in *Java* than by trying out Greenfoot. There are lots of free resources on this site including many great video tutorials.

http://www.greenfoot.org/

Appendix

Some key bits of information

Companion website

Go to www.codingclub.co.uk for the complete source code to all the apps in this book plus example answers for many of the puzzles, challenges and ideas found at the end of each chapter. Also find out about the characters that feature in the books and other exciting information about the *Coding Club* series. While on the website, take the time to submit your email address to 'keep informed' about the latest developments as and when they happen.

Useful code examples

while loops:

```python
while my_test == True:
    # code that does things goes here
```

for loops:

```python
for i in my_list:
    print(i)
```

quick comparison function:

```python
def is_same(guess, password):
    return guess == password
    # returns True if the same and False if different
```

tkinter window template:

```python
from tkinter import *

# order a window from the tkinter factory
window = Tk()
window.title("My Application")

# other code goes here #

# start the animation loop
window.mainloop()
```

class example:

```python
# code in file called cat.py
class Cat:
    # constructor:
    def __init__(self, name):
        self.name = name

    # other methods
    def speak(self):
        print(self.name, " says Meow!")

    def drink(self):
        print(self.name, " drinks some milk.")
```

instantiation example:

```
import cat
romeo = cat.Cat("Romeo")
```

Class planning template

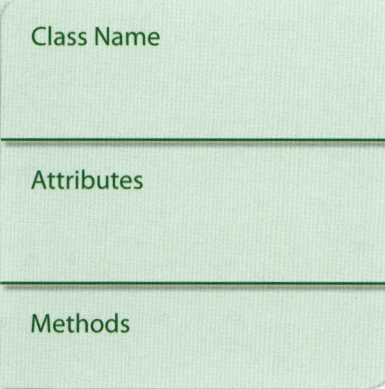

(A printable version is available on the companion website.)

Glossary and index

argument   a piece of information that is required by a function, a method or a class so that it can perform its task; this is usually a **string** or number, for example, `my_function(arguments go here)`.   11

attributes   the properties of an object such as width, height, colour, etc.   27

boolean variable   a variable that holds only two values – `True` or `False`   11

bug   a piece of code that is causing a program to fail to run properly or at all   48

casting   the process of converting one data-type into another; for example, sometimes a number may be stored as text but need to be converted in to an integer; this can be done like this: `int("3")`   99

classes   in object-oriented programming, classes are sections of code that objects are built from; in this book they are compared to factories although it is more common to describe them as templates or blueprints   19

comments   some text in a computer program that is for the human reader and is ignored by the computer when running the program; in python all comments begin with a hash symbol #   9

comparative operators	sometimes called logic operators, they allow us to compare data in a program; they include == and >	14
concatenating	the joining of two strings into one string	99
constant	a number that does not change; it is good practice to name constants in capitals e.g. `SPEED_OF_LIGHT`	10
constructor	a special kind of method that is called when an instance of a class is created; it is constructed with the Python keyword `__init__`; one of its purposes is to initialise an object's attributes	23
data-types	different types of information stored by the computer, for example floats, integers, strings, tuples, lists and dictionaries	99
debugging	the process of finding bugs in a program	48
default value	a value given to an argument or variable as a starting point	29
dot operator	a dot is used in coding to link a method or function with its class or module e.g. in `math.random(1,6)` the dot tells the computer that the random function is found in the math module	14
equals operator	the equals sign is used to assign a value to a variable in coding, for example `n=2` assigns the value 2 to the variable `n`	10

factory	in this book, factory is used to describe a class (in advanced object-oriented programming the word has a different meaning)	19
function	a reusable piece of code	10
global variable	a variable that is usable anywhere in a program	63
hacking	taking some previously written code and re-writing bits to make it do something different	49
hard coded	when an actual value is put into code instead of a variable that can subsequently change e.g. `width = 45` is hard coded whereas `width = my_width_variable` is not	50
IDE	stands for Integrated Development Environment; IDLE is an example of one; they are special text editors with useful tools built in for programmers	8
IDLE	stands for Integrated DeveLopment Environment; this is the IDE that comes with a normal Python 3 install	8
index	the number that references a value in a string, tuple or list; each item in the container data type is indexed from 0 for the first item, 1 for the next etc.	85
infinite loop	a piece of code that keeps running forever; this is usually a bad thing	63
initialise	to assign a start value to a variable	27

instance	in object-oriented programming, an instance is an object created from a class	22
instantiate[d]	in object-oriented programming the process of bringing into existence an object created from a class	22
interactive mode	this is when we use IDLE to try out snippets of code without saving them	8
lists	ordered container data types that can hold values of any type and can have elements added or removed; like tuples each element is indexed from 0	106
local variable	a variable that is defined inside a function and is only usable inside that function	63
loop	a piece of code that keeps repeating until a certain condition is met	47
method	the name given to a function in a class	20
module	a saved Python file whose functions can be used by another program	10
objects	in object-oriented programming, objects are instances of classes – entities created from factories e.g. lion is an object instantiated from the Cat class	18
object-oriented programming (OOP)	a system of programming where the emphasis is on building objects from classes rather than focusing on actions and logic	17
parameters	another name for attributes	27

return	(1) the value a function will produce after it has been run (it is also a Python keyword) and (2) the 'end of line' key on a keyboard, sometimes called the enter key	11
script mode	this is when we use IDLE to help us write code that we will save in a file	8
statement	used in this book to mean a snippet of code; strictly speaking it is a piece of code that represents a command or action, e.g. a print statement	21
string	text data, which can be stored in a variable	10
tkinter	a package of classes that are often imported in to Python programs that give methods that are useful for producing windows, drawing images and producing animations	19
tuple	an ordered container data type whose values are indexed from 0; its contents cannot be changed	85
values	information that can be stored in a variable, such as the elements in a container data type	11
variable	a name that refers to a place in a computer's memory where data is stored; more loosely, it can also be used to refer to that data	8
while loop	a kind of loop that repeats code while a comparative statement returns `True`	13

The Quick Quiz answers

Quick Quiz 2.1

The `random` module was imported in the Chapter 1 app.

Quick Quiz 3.1

The table we will get will have no net because the default settings are `vertical_net=False` and `horizontal_net=False`. This is so that we have to choose to have a net when ordering a table.

Quick Quiz 3.2

```
my_table = table.Table(window, vertical_net=True, width=600, height=400,
                       colour="blue", net_colour="red")
```

Quick Quiz 5.1

Answer A is correct. We have not ordered any bats in `main.py`. This comes next.

Acknowledgements

It is a weird transformation that a would-be author goes through when trying to obtain the support of a publisher. While trying to find a company's support, you wonder why no one can see the brilliance of your idea – of course it will make millions! On obtaining the support of a publisher you quickly see all the hard work it involves, the investment of time and money and the number of people involved. Suddenly it is impossible not to become eternally grateful! Special thanks go to Paraminder Dhillon, Carl Saxton and Heather Mahy at Cambridge University Press for all their help with this book.

Special thanks must also go to Alex Bradbury for his technical advice on this edition and his patience with my insistence that classes are better described as factories rather than blueprints or templates.

The characters have all aged three years and new ones have joined the club. Thanks to Fran again for the great drawings, I love the way José has turned into such a fashion conscious teenager!

The authors and publishers acknowledge the following sources of copyright material and are grateful for the permissions granted.

p. 7 Stephen VanHorn/Shutterstock; p. 18 by permission of McLaren Automotive Ltd; p. 27 Nuno Andre/Shutterstock; p. 33 Andrey Burmakin/Shutterstock

The publisher has used its best endeavours to ensure that the URLs for external websites referred to in this book are correct and active at the time of going to press. However, the publisher has no responsibility for the websites and can make no guarantee that a site will remain live or that the content is or will remain appropriate.